BARRIE MEYER
GETTING IT RIGHT

BARRIE MEYER
GETTING IT RIGHT

BARRIE MEYER
WITH ANDREW HIGNELL

TEMPUS

First published 2006

Tempus Publishing Limited
The Mill, Brimscombe Port,
Stroud, Gloucestershire, GL5 2QG
www.tempus-publishing.com

British Library Cataloguing in Publication Data.
A catalogue record for this book is available from the British Library.

ISBN 0 7524 4007 1

Typesetting and origination by Tempus Publishing Limited
Printed in Great Britain

Contents

Acknowledgements

This book could not have been written had it not been for the kind help of Barrie, his wife Glenda, Laura Heapy and other members of Barrie's family, as well as the late Rita Clive who was the first to encourage Barrie in collating his memoirs. I'm very grateful to all of them for producing a superb collection of evocative memories, as well as many treasured personal items that have been reproduced in this book. My thanks also to Holly Bennion and Rob Sharman of Tempus Publishing for their enthusiastic support and encouragement as this book has taken shape. I would also like to thank the following for their kind assistance as well – Keith Gerrish, Mike Simpson, David Foot, David Green, Kim Stuckey, Mike Jay, Ray Taylor, Roger Skyrme, Roy Palmer, David Constant, Ray Julian, Merv Kitchen, Alan Whitehead, John Higson, Tom Richardson and also my wife, Debra, for helping proofread the final manuscript, and supporting me throughout this project.

Andrew Hignell

Introduction

Barrie Meyer was the second county umpire I ever met – the first was David Evans, who was the father of Neil, one of my friends at school in Cardiff when I was growing up in the late 1960s and early 1970s. David had umpired in some of our school games and helped at our practices and training sessions. Also, when I reached the final of our school 'Mastermind' competition, it was David who set the questions on my specialist subject – the history of Glamorgan CCC.

I'd spoken to David several times when he was standing in a county match at Cardiff or Swansea and, on one of my visits to watch Glamorgan play, David introduced me to Barrie, who was standing in the game. Only a few weeks before, David had sat alongside my father at a parents' evening, and he'd clearly found out a little bit more about the lad who, at the drop of a hat, liked to head off from school to watch the county games at Sophia Gardens. Having found out from my father that I had been born in Gloucester, David, or Mr Evans as I deferentially called him, said to Barrie, 'This is Andrew – he's at school with my son, and he's a clever lad as he follows Glamorgan, despite having been born in Gloucestershire!'

Barrie responded with a smile, a handshake and a few words of encouragement. 'What a nice chap,' I thought after our brief conversation ended and I headed back to sit with my other friends in the members' enclosure feeling ten feet tall. I don't expect Barrie to remember our first meeting, especially as neither of us thought that thirty years later, I would be helping 'Mr Meyer' to assemble his memoirs.

But those first few words of encouragement have remained in my memory, and I'm glad to say that, after helping to collate his recollections, those first impressions about Barrie Meyer when a schoolboy in Cardiff over thirty years ago, have remained the same – what a nice fellow he is.

Andrew Hignell
St Fagans, Cardiff
February 2006

ONE

Umpire-Chumpire: Are we a Dying Breed?

'Barrie Meyer? Oh yes, he's the cricket umpire who gave Viv Richards out and then apologised to him for making an incorrect decision.' That's what I've heard many times, and so have my friends and colleagues over the past twenty years or so. Add to this the headline of 'Chumpire', which accompanied a photograph in *The Sun* newspaper in May 1989 for the one-day international between England and Australia, compounded by the words 'Aussie rage at let-off for Gooch' above the tabloid's match report.

It was reading things like this and overhearing comments about the Viv Richards decision that made me start to wonder whether umpires are a dying breed, and if my fourteen years playing for Gloucestershire followed by twenty-five years as a first-class umpire have been wasted. But then I think about all the good times – the rewarding days that brought me not only the satisfaction of a job competently done, but having the sheer joy of watching, and being involved with, innumerable top-class batsmen, fielders, bowlers and wicketkeepers.

Add to that the bank of experience I have acquired over the years and passed on to fellow umpires, as well as being in a position to see and use the electronic aids that have helped to raise the accuracy of an umpiring decision. Umpires are definitely an integral part of the game, and no, we are not a dying breed.

So what was it that led to those comments and words above that made me ask those questions? Well, it all began during the series between England and the West Indies, and the Test match at Lord's at the end of June 1984, when I stood with the late David Evans – another former professional cricketer who, like myself, was a wicketkeeper on the county circuit before swapping the gloves and pads for the umpire's white coat.

England had batted first, making 286 with Graeme Fowler, the Lancashire batsman, scoring a composed 106 while Chris Broad, his opening partner, compiled 55 against the fine West Indies attack, spearheaded by the late Malcolm Marshall. Like England's Ian Botham, who also gave a fine display of swing bowling when the tourists batted, Marshall could swing and seam the ball with some pace. In fact, the match saw David Evans and myself give twelve lbw decisions – an indication of the extent of the movement of the ball and the difficulties that the batsmen encountered. Indeed, it was when Botham was bowling that my decision that stirred up a real hornets' nest came about. Viv Richards was batting superbly and had scored 72, when Ian Botham delivered one that swung sharply into him. Having started to play a shot, Viv changed his mind and opted to play no stroke at all. The ball then hit him right in front of the stumps, and the appeals rang out from the England team.

But, as I raised my finger to give Viv out leg before, the appeals suddenly stopped. I immediately thought that there was something strange about this and I quickly realised that I had made a massive blunder because, with the lavish swing, the ball was likely to have missed leg stump. Viv stood there for a moment before walking off to the pavilion, and my immediate intention was to call Viv back to continue his innings. But I decided not to do this because the non-striker Clive Lloyd – the West Indies captain – had turned and made his way back to the crease, and I did not want the players or crowd to think that I had been influenced or intimidated by Clive, so I let it go. However, I walked across to David Evans, my colleague at square-leg, and told him that I thought I had made a terrible mistake. His advice was short and simple – forget about it and get on with the game.

But the incident continued to prey on my mind and, during the lunch interval, I knocked on the door of the West Indian dressing room and asked to go in to speak to Viv. He was sitting on the balcony and, as I walked across the room, the other players looked at me as if to say, 'Hello – is there a problem here?', as if they thought that I would have something to say to Viv about the reaction that he had shown at his dismissal. I went up to him and said, 'Viv, I made a terrible mistake out there. I don't know what came over me, and I just want you to know that I'm sorry.' Viv looked up at me from his chair and replied, 'No problem man, no problem at all,' which I felt showed the character of the man.

The West Indies were bowled out for 245 and, for a while, it looked as if my wrong decision was going to have a big influence on the game. England then replied with 300 for 9 before David Gower declared at 11.20 a.m. on the final day and invited the West Indies to chase 342 to win. They only had around five hours at their disposal, and few sides had ever achieved anything like that to win on the final day. But the tourists accepted the challenge and responded with a magnificent display of batting, particularly from Gordon Greenidge, who ended up unbeaten on 214. He was ably supported by Larry Gomes, who made an unbeaten 92 as the West Indies reached 344 for 1 wicket, to win the game with 11.5 of the last 20 overs to spare.

It had been a magnificent game of cricket but, unfortunately for me, there was a terrific amount of publicity – not about my decision to give Viv his marching orders, but because I had subsequently apologised to him for my incorrect decision. At the end of the day's play, I had been sitting with my wife and a group of friends on a low wall facing the main entrance of the Lord's pavilion. Graham Otway, a member of the Press, came up and asked me if it was true that I had apologised to Viv for my incorrect decision, and he asked if he could mention this in his report. I agreed to this and added wryly that the Press were bound to crucify me anyway. Our party then left Lord's and headed for the Cricketers Club of London where many famous cricketers have enjoyed the hospitality and unwound in the convivial setting off Baker Street. It was there that I was approached by two other pressmen, Peter Smith and Michael Carey – for both of whom I had the utmost of respect. They each expressed some concern for me, because they told me that they had also heard the apology story and that they had no option but to print it. They also expressed the opinion that I should not have apologised to Viv.

Some time later I was summoned to Lord's by Donald Carr, the secretary of the Test and County Cricket Board (TCCB), in order to explain the incident involving Viv to him. I then received what can be called a reprimand as he considered that I could be setting a precedent by apologising to a player. David Whiley from the Association of Cricket Umpires (ACU) also expressed a similar point of view.

But what about my point of view? I had squared my conscience and I considered that I had done the honourable thing. Human beings are just that – human, and I believe in the axiom that to err is human and to forgive divine. My action at Lord's that day certainly caused a few shockwaves to ripple through the cricketing world. The initial reaction of the Press was to criticise me severely, while it was clear from the secretaries of the TCCB and ACU that I had set a precedent, and that the purists of the game would be shocked.

Useful error

'I MAY have made a mistake,' said umpire Barry Meyer about his decision to give West Indies star batsman Viv Richards out in the Test match last Saturday.

This admission of error was so unusual that it took people's breath away. It certainly removed any rancour felt by Richards's fans. Indeed the forthright declaration that he may have got it wrong seems to have made him friends. Why should this be ?

Perhaps because everyone boobs some time and we all feel a sense of relief when someone else makes a howler since we no longer feel alone. We even have a sense of gratitude to those who admit to making fools of themselves.

One day politicians will realise the vote-winning possibilities of public penance.

But not for some time yet: it's hard to break the habit of a lifetime — of always being in the right.

The editorial from the *Daily Mail*.

But in an interview with the *Daily Star*, Viv Richards took a different point of view, saying, 'It took a lot of courage for him to admit that he was wrong in giving me out lbw in the first innings of the Lord's Test this week… He's had the guts to come right out and say that he made an error. We've always known him as a good umpire. Now we also know he's an honest man too.' The West Indies captain, Clive Lloyd, also told Pat Gibson of the *Daily Express* that 'the replays suggested that the ball was missing the leg stump, but we have to accept the decision as we do all umpiring decisions. And you can only admire a man who is big enough to admit that he made a mistake.'

In August 1985 I had another encounter with the media during the NatWest Trophy semi-final between Hampshire and Essex at Southampton. By a strange quirk of fate, it occurred on my birthday — 21 August — and it happened shortly after Graham Gooch had reached his half-century. He was batting superbly at the time, and quickly went for a single after getting to fifty. I got into the right position, square of the wicket but, as Gooch ran his bat in, it created a cloud of dust that obscured my view. The ball came in quickly from the fielder and there was an appeal for run out, but I couldn't see the batting line clearly because of the dust created by Gooch's bat. The cardinal rule is when in doubt give the batsman the benefit, so I shook my head and, in this age before the introduction of third umpires, said not out.

However, the TV replay showed that Gooch was out, and when the game went into the second day, this particular incident involving Gooch was shown again before the start of play. Mark Nicholas, the fielding captain, was also interviewed, and asked about what he thought of the incident. I was very grateful for the tactful way that Mark handled the question, stating that an umpire's job is a difficult one, and that we had to make instant decisions without having the immediate advantage that television replays can produce.

Essex went on to win the game, with Gooch scoring an unbeaten 93, and in September they won the final of the knock-out competition, which I also officiated with David Constant. It was a magnificent game of cricket with Gooch scoring 91 and Brian Hardie 110. Their efforts helped Essex post a good total of 280 for 2, before Derek Randall led a spirited run-chase with a fine innings of 66. We were set for a tremendous finish with Derek Pringle bowling the final over of the game at my end, with Randall on strike and Nottinghamshire needing 18 to win. He took 16 runs off the first 5 deliveries but, with the last ball of the game, Pringle succeeded in tucking Randall up, as he again tried to move inside the ball, and Paul Prichard took a catch at mid-wicket to give Essex victory by 1 run.

I was able to live with my 'mistake' over Gooch in the semi-final but four years later came another incident involving the England and Essex batsman, when my integrity as an umpire was questioned. It happened during the Texaco Trophy one-day international between England and Australia on 29 May, 1989. It could have been the final straw because this was when, the day after the game, the newspaper reports carried the headline 'Chumpire', with a freeze-frame photograph showing Gooch just short of his ground. At the time, there were no television replays for line decisions and in the instant that I had to make the decision, I honestly thought that Gooch had just made his ground. Soon after the game, David Frith, the editor of *Wisden Cricket Monthly*, spoke to me about the incident and asked me about the viability of a third umpire watching television replays.

At the time, I was chairman of the First-Class Umpires' Panel and, at our next meeting, I duly raised the issue with them. The majority of

my colleagues were loath to agree with this idea, as they felt they had
to make decisions out in the field, and they would stand by those decisions. Having television replays, they felt, would be an intrusion and the
game would suffer as a consequence. However, I believed differently, perhaps because of the three incidents above, that it would be advantageous
to the standing umpires to have a third official watching a replay monitor, who could play their part in making line decisions, and when there
had been a question mark as to the legality of a fielder stopping a ball on the
boundary.

But I knew from my own experience that there had been times in the
past when the television replays are not helpful at all. An example came in
the Roses Match in May 1980, when I umpired the televised game between
Yorkshire and Lancashire at Headingley. One of the commentators was my
good friend Michael Carey, who lived near me in Derbyshire. At the end
of the day's play on the Saturday we travelled back home in Michael's car,
and we discussed the day's play, which had seen Lancashire make 234, before
Yorkshire's openers Geoff Boycott and Richard Lumb went in to face the
final few overs of the day. Willie Hogg was bowling from my end and he
bowled a beauty to Boycott, who just got a nick on it and was caught by
Chris Scott, the wicketkeeper.

Michael's first comment to me was, 'Did you have a good day today?' to
which I replied that, as far as I could recall, everything went okay. 'What
about the Boycott dismissal?' he then asked. 'It was a clear-cut decision,'
I said, but Michael then told me that the replays he had watched in the
commentary box had shown that Boycott had not touched the ball. I stated
firmly that I knew that he had hit it, and on the Monday morning before
the start of play, Michael and I asked the television engineers to replay the
incident. When initially played at full speed, I could not believe what I saw
because the screen showed a gap of less than an inch between bat and ball.
I could still not accept this, as I was still adamant that Boycott had touched
the ball, so I asked the engineer to play it in slow motion – this time the
gap was much narrower, but nevertheless, there was still a gap. Then the
engineer played something that the public were not normally shown, the
frame-by-frame sequence. Ten frames were replayed and, on one of the ten,
the ball had just connected with the top corner of Boycott's bat.

I was delighted – I am quite willing to admit when I am wrong, but I am
also adamant when I know, based on my cricketing instincts and what I've
seen or heard, that I made a correct decision. Michael quickly apologised

and said that the decision was correct and, later in his commentary that day, he told the viewers that any doubts on Saturday over Boycott's dismissal had been erased by these replays, which showed that the England batsman had indeed edged the ball to the wicketkeeper.

We now live in an age with far more advanced technology, and innovations such as the 'super slow-mo' and 'snickometer' have vastly improved the quality of the replays, giving much clearer and sharper images to the benefit of everyone involved in or watching the game.

Third and fourth officials have therefore been successfully introduced for all televised games, and thankfully there have been no more headlines like 'Chumpire'. The replay umpires are in a better position to assess a marginal line decision and, I'm glad to say, the introduction of a third umpire has not eroded the authority of the on-field team – something that my colleagues in the late 1980s and early 1990s were particularly concerned about. Other innovations have also been added, such as 'Hawkeye', and using these have helped the training of new umpires, especially for situations when they will be standing in games when no television cameras are present, so that they will hopefully assess the situation correctly, and make the right decision.

As far as I was concerned back in the 1980s and 1990s, it wasn't very pleasant at the time to read the headlines and newspaper reports, and to see the images of incidents where I had apparently made a mistake. But now, as I look back over my career, I realise that I was involved in the game at an important time in its evolution, and perhaps my errors and the adverse publicity they caused proved to cricket's authorities that the technological innovations had to be embraced.

TWO

Growing up in Bournemouth

I was born in Bournemouth into a footballing family – the second son of Walter Bertram Meyer and Alice Emily Violet Meyer – on 21 August 1932. My father was a bus driver and a decent amateur footballer with the Bournemouth Transport club, and his brother was a professional with the Bournemouth & Boscombe Athletic side, so I guess soccer was in my blood. To be quite frank, I never thought as a young boy of doing anything else with my life apart from playing football. Cricket was what you played in the summer when it was too hot to play football!

In fact, one of my earliest memories involves playing football when, at the age of three, I literally had a smashing time. We were sitting in our house in Washington Avenue, Bournemouth and my father was juggling a soft rubber ball in his hands. He then threw me the ball, but was a bit short in his aim. It bounced in front of me and with my right foot I struck it perfectly on the half-volley. It flew across the room but, unfortunately, it went straight into a beautiful Swiss clock, which was one of my mother's prized possessions, and the clock was smashed into smithereens. It seemed then that I had perfect ball sense even at that age, although my mother did not hold the same view about my prowess!

Not long after, I started at a kindergarten school in a nearby street and, on one particular day, my older brother Kenneth came to fetch me with a scarf that my mother said I should wear for the short walk home. I gather that I had an opposite view about the scarf, and strenuously rejected Ken's efforts to make me wear it. So much so in fact that, when he tried to grab me, I ran away from him, straight into the road and into the path of a local taxi. The car braked sharply but still hit me and, as it was raining at the time, I was fortunately pushed along the wet surface of the road, rather than being run over. I was duly taken off to hospital with a broken collarbone and severe shock, but I was not the only one in shock – my mother, who was pregnant at the time, also went into trauma after being told about my accident, and tragically lost her third child.

My collarbone soon mended and, in a year or so, I graduated to St Clements Junior School. I was no different to the other young boys at the school, enjoying all sorts of ball games in the playground, eagerly collecting and swapping cigarette cards and getting into further scrapes. One of these involved scrumping apples from the branches of any trees that we could reach. On one occasion I had to scramble up a picket fence with wire at the top in order to pinch the apples but, just as I grabbed some of the fruit, I lost my balance and fell. Unfortunately my right heel got stuck in the wire and I went head first straight onto the pavement. I hit the ground with an almighty bump and, after being dazed for a few seconds, I got up and ran off. By the time I got home I had stopped seeing stars but I had a lump on my forehead about the size of an egg. I couldn't tell my father what had happened for fear of not being allowed out to play with my friends, so I made up a white lie, hoping that I would at least get a bit of sympathy. But I got none at all and, to this day, I think my father had an inkling about what my friends and I had been up to and knew that the best punishment was to give me no sympathy whatsoever!

It was round about this time that I started to ask my parents for a bicycle. My father would say 'Well, we can't afford it,' – he was probably right because I can remember how, early on a Friday morning, I was sent out to stand at the bus stop at the top of our street so that when his bus passed I could go back home with his weekly wage packet and give it to my mother so that she could go out and do some shopping. We weren't a very wealthy family, so I had to think of another way of raising the cash for my bicycle. Each week, my parents would buy me two comics – *Adventure* and the *Dandy*. Many of my friends at school were worse off than us, and didn't even get any comics at all, so I decided to take them into school and sold them for half a penny each. Over time, my little stock of pennies began to build up and, with regular reminders about what I wanted, my parents gave in and put my pennies towards the purchase of a bicycle. But only a few weeks after I had first ridden my prized bike, disaster struck again as I made my way home along the main road from the local shops. My mother had given me a shopping bag that, on the way down, I had thrown over the handlebars of the bike but, on the way back, the weight of the groceries unbalanced the bike and made me swerve violently to the right. I fell off, and was just picking myself up when, to my horror, a trolley bus came along and ran over my bicycle. The poor thing was twisted into such a dreadful shape that it was only fit for the scrap yard and, although I was not hurt in falling off, I was in tears for many days afterwards, pining for my dear little bicycle.

As far as my days at St Clements were concerned, I did what was necessary at school but I was never one for serious academic study – perhaps as a result of a teacher at the school who had a rather strict approach and was not averse to inflicting pain on his pupils. He used to slowly walk in between the desks, looking over the shoulders of his pupils, and I can still remember how, now and again, I would get a couple of smacks with a ruler on my knuckles because of some unknown failing. On a few occasions he also pinched me above the ear and tried to pull me up from my chair. What I had done wrong I still don't know, but his sadistic manner nearly put me off school altogether – thank God that sort of thing no longer happens. At the age of eleven I started to attend Boscombe Secondary School. It had three streams and, despite my experiences at St Clements, I was placed into the top grade. I'm glad to say that I remained there as sport really took hold of me and I became captain of my year's football and cricket team. In those days at Boscombe, I was a fast-bowling all-rounder, and I can remember taking 5 for 12 in one match, and hitting a match-winning 77 not out in another important game.

But I was soccer mad, and the only thing that was in my thoughts at the time was being a professional footballer. As well as scrumping apples, I would gleefully gather up any tennis balls that had been hit over the fencing surrounding the courts near where my friends and I played. I would then take the balls home and store them in the back garden so that, on my walk to school, I could dribble the ball along the pavement and now and again plant it into a hedge, pretending that I was scoring the match-winning goal.

My parents soon knew of my love for football, as the toe of my right shoe would quickly get scuffed before splitting open. My mother didn't complain about the number of shoes I was going through and, one Christmas, my parents bought me a brand-new leather football – the sort that had an inner tube that, first of all, you had to blow up before covering it up with the leather and lacing the ball up. I would proudly take the ball with me for games of football with my friends in Kings Park, right next to Dean

Boscombe Secondary School six-a-side football team.

Court, the home of Bournemouth & Boscombe Football Club. There was a bank with a road on top running through the park, so we would pitch our goal up against the steep bank. But bad luck struck again, as one shot from my friend sent the ball right up the bank and onto the road. I had been in goal and, after diving and missing the ball, I watched in horror as an Army lorry then came along the road and ran over the ball, bursting the inner tube. Once again, I went home in floods of tears with a ruined Christmas present!

On Saturday afternoons, my love of football was fuelled further as my brother and I went to Dean Court, where Kenneth had secured a job with Bournemouth & Boscombe FC, selling programmes. It gave us the opportunity to get into the Cherries' games for free, although we usually missed the first quarter of an hour as we were still selling programmes around the ground, or to latecomers. But it gave us the chance to watch some League football, and we soon got to know several of the players – one called Paddy Gallacher would even bring us back a programme from the away games.

During the summer, my friends and I would also go down to the beach at Boscombe with a bottle of pop, chocolate, sandwiches and, needless to say, some tennis balls and a football. It was great fun playing football on the beach, and a few of the American soldiers who were taking in the sea air would regularly come and join us. They also shared their chewing gum and candy with us, and one day they even taught us the rudiments of baseball. Less enjoyable, though, was the time when I went off with a few older friends for a walk along the foreshore. They took me along a submerged sandbank sticking out into the sea. As we went further and further from the shore, I began to find myself getting out of my depth. My taller friends were alright, but I slipped, lost my balance and fell into the sea. I quickly lost my bearings and, to make matters worse, I wasn't a very strong swimmer. I only just made it back to the shore, and went straight back home sopping wet and rather chastened after quite a frightening experience.

At the age of fourteen I was old enough to leave Boscombe Secondary School. There were two options open to me – one was to continue my education by sitting an entrance exam for Canford School, the famous public school near Bournemouth, while the other was to go out into the world and get a job. Well, I opted for the latter and went one weekend for an interview with G.E. and W.R.J. Lambert, a building firm in Winton, about five miles from home. At the end of the interview, they offered me the post of junior clerk. I accepted and the terms were agreed – my salary was the princely sum of £1 a week, out of which I had to pay 4*d* for a stamp on the National Health.

I went home and told my parents who were, I remember, rather flabbergasted. They had no knowledge of what I had arranged until I went home and told them. Maybe they wanted me to go to Canford, but I had decided otherwise and, shortly afterwards, I reported for duty to Mr James, the office manager. He carefully outlined what my duties were to be – answering phone calls and operating the switchboard, taking charge of the stationery cupboard, making tea for between six and ten people, and being in charge of the post, including putting letters into envelopes, putting on the stamps and taking the mail to the post office. None of these duties needed a lot of grey matter, but I felt that I had joined the real world, and a measure of my satisfaction and success in the post was that I stayed with the company for the next three years, and received a pay rise of an extra pound a week in my second year, and again in my third year.

Having a wage of £3 a week was quite good money, and I was also able to start playing a good standard of football on Saturday afternoon. By this time I had joined Pokesdown Youth Club, having met some boys down in Kings Park who, having seen me play football, suggested that I joined the club, which was a six-mile cycle ride away from my home. It was quite a successful social club and I enjoyed every minute that I was there. It had several sports fields, a snooker room, a table-tennis lounge, a canteen and a dance floor. My parents had agreed to my joining the club, and it was not long before I had made many new friends, including Glynn Gubb, whose parents owned a fish and chip shop in Boscombe. Glynn and I called into their shop on our bike ride back to Boscombe, and his parents were always very kind and generous, giving me free fish and chips before I headed home.

The Pokesdown Youth Club also had a decent football team, and I was pleased to get a place in their team soon, at inside left. I scored several goals and had clearly made a mark with them and, in 1948/49, I was chosen for the Hampshire Boys' Club in the national knockout competition against other county teams and regional sides. We beat Buckinghamshire and Berkshire, as well as Devon & Cornwall, with my tally of goals rising to half a dozen after we also defeated the London Association of Boys' Clubs by the margin of 7-2 in the semi-final.

The final was at The Valley, the home of Charlton Athletic, with our opponents being Lancashire. The game was on a Saturday morning, so I had to arrange time off, but sadly it was to no avail, as the Lancashire lads beat us. This match was also on the same day as the final of a local competition that the Pokesdown Club had reached. So, after playing up in London, I quickly got changed, made my way to Paddington station to catch the train home, and then got a car to pick me up to take me to Dean Park. I just managed to get there in time for kick-off, but the same result happened as in the morning, and I went home at the end of a long day, wondering how many other aspiring footballers had lost in the finals of two competitions on the same day!

THREE

Football with Bristol Rovers

My success at inside left and my goalscoring record with the Hampshire Boys' team had not gone unnoticed, and I felt really honoured when I was told that I had been chosen in the England Boys' Clubs team to play Wales at Wrexham. It was a long train journey to north Wales, but I was very proud to receive my cap, and also to play alongside several other lads who had already signed professional terms. Even better, I managed to score a goal, and the English lads won 3-1.

My goalscoring had also attracted the attention of several League clubs, as I discovered one day when I was ill at home with tonsillitis. I was upstairs in bed, feeling rather glum as it looked as though my swollen glands might stop me from playing football at the weekend. Anyhow, I remember a knock at the door downstairs and I heard my father answering it. My ears really pricked up when I heard the caller introducing himself by saying that he was Mr Hyde, the chief scout from Bristol Rovers Football Club, and that he had been trying to track me down for about three weeks. Apparently, Mr Hyde had heard of my goalscoring record: 47 goals in 32 games for the Pokesdown Club, as well as my success with the Hampshire side. He had been told by someone that I lived in Southampton, but had initially met with no success in tracking me down. My good friend Glynn Gubb had also been chosen in the Hampshire side, and I think it was through Glynn that Mr Hyde arrived at my home in Washington Avenue. I could hear Mr Hyde and my father talking downstairs for a few minutes, and then my father came up to my bedroom. 'There's a chappie downstairs called Fred Hyde,' he said. 'He wants you to come and have trials with Bristol Rovers Football Club.' My tonsillitis improved considerably from that moment onwards!

I was really thrilled at the age of seventeen to travel up to Bristol with my father to have trials for Bristol Rovers. The original date they had suggested had clashed with my brother Kenneth's wedding, so Fred Hyde arranged instead for me to go the following week, when many of the club's playing staff were taking part in a trial match. It was quite a baptism, especially as most of the other players in the match were full-time professionals. I had known beforehand that it was going to be quite tough, so I wasn't expecting much after the game when I went with my father to the office of Brough Fletcher, the Rovers manager. By coincidence, my father and Brough had served in the same regiment in India during the First World War, so at first they swapped a few old jokes and stories about their times together. Then Brough took my breath away, firstly by offering me professional terms there and then on the spot, and secondly by telling me the terms – £10 to sign the forms, £7 a week in the winter and £5 a week in the summer, plus bonuses of £2 for every League win and £1 for a draw.

On the way home, I thought I was in a dream, especially as I believed that, at £3 a week, I was on very good money with Lamberts Builders. As soon as I got home, I told my mother the wonderful news, and we started planning for my move to Bristol. Given Bournemouth's popularity as a seaside resort, we had started to take in a few guests for bed and breakfast, and one of our regulars were a family called the Summerills who lived in Hanham.

My parents wrote to them asking them to suggest decent digs in Bristol, but they immediately replied, suggesting that I instead lived with them in Hanham. So, in October 1949, I made my way to Bristol to live with Bert and Betty, plus their three daughters Beryl, Molly and Jackie.

I was initially a member of the Rovers' Colts team that played in the Western League, and I also turned out a few times in the Downs League for Sneyd Park. I only scored 4 goals in 12 matches for the Colts, and we only won 4 games, but I had done enough for our new manager, Bert Tann, to promote me into the reserve XI in January 1950. I had 14 games for the reserves for the rest of the season, scoring only 3 times, but we won 7 of those matches and drew a further 3. The start of the 1950/51 season saw me in the reserves again and, in the opening few matches, we continued our decent run of form from the previous season. I had only scored a couple of goals when, one day, Bert Tann called me into his office. I wondered at first if he was going to have a chat with me about my form but, to my surprise, he told me that I would be in the Rovers' first team for the home match against Bournemouth on 7 October.

Needless to say I was thrilled at this news, and I immediately went off to ring my parents. They subsequently sent a telegram saying that they were arranging to travel to Bristol to watch the match so, for the next few days at training, I ensured that I didn't pick up a knock. Come Saturday morning the butterflies were fluttering overtime in my stomach but, as soon as I got changed, I felt more relaxed and, by the time I ran out with the rest of the team, in front of some 18,000 spectators, I felt quite confident. The atmosphere of a League game was completely new to me, but I just focused on my job and, to the delight of my parents, I scored one of the goals as we beat my home-town side 2-0. It came five minutes from the end of the contest, as I received a pass from Vic Lambdon, beat two defenders and, from about six yards out, placed the ball into the corner of the goal. I was mobbed by the whole of the Bristol side, and a huge roar went around the ground as all of my colleagues came up to congratulate me.

Mr Tann, and the journalists with the local newspapers, thought that I had had a good game, so I kept my place for the next match, away to Exeter City. We won 2-0 again, but I picked up a nasty injury, as Ray Goddard, the centre half, got his foot tangled up with my ankle. The upshot was that I was out for six weeks with torn ligaments, and I was only just back in training in January 1951 when my call-up came to do two years of national service. I was attached to the Army's Royal Ordnance Corps, and had to report to Aldershot for an initial training course of some thirteen weeks. During this time I didn't get a chance to play much football but, once I had completed this course, I was transferred to the Hilsea Barracks in Portsmouth, and was allowed weekend leave to play for Bristol Rovers.

While at Hilsea I also got plenty of exercise in the week, as the battalion team were in a successful cup run in an Army competition. Several of their earlier games had also been postponed so, by the time I joined them, they had several games to catch up on and, for several weeks, I didn't even put on a uniform, as Major Smith and Corporal Jackson ensured that we prepared for these cup matches by having regular training sessions and eating better food than others at the barracks.

It was also while at Hilsea that I kept wicket for the first time. After a couple of net sessions, I was put into the battalion's cricket XI and asked if I would keep wicket. I'd never kept before in my life but I reasoned that by keeping wicket I wouldn't have to do Army duties instead so I said yes. As it turned out I didn't find it too difficult, and I also managed to score a century as well in one of the battalion's games.

For the 1951/52 football season, the battalion were entered into the Hampshire League so, once again, I took part in regular matches during the week, while also getting weekend leave to play for the Rovers. There were five other professional footballers in the battalion, so we had quite a useful team, losing just 9 of the 51 games that we played. I also managed to get into the Southern Command team for a couple of matches, playing alongside Jackie Henderson, the Scottish international who was playing for Portsmouth. It would be true to say therefore that, during my national service, I spent more time in either football kit or cricket whites than in my soldier's uniform.

I returned to Bristol Rovers in January 1953, and my new 'digs' with Les and Joan Allen, who had an off-licence behind the Rovers' ground at Eastville. Naturally, I was eager to win a regular place in their first team. While with the Army I had played a few more times for the first team, but most of my games had been for the reserve side in the Football Combination. For the rest of the 1952/53 season I was not a regular member of the first team, who won promotion into the Second Division of the English League.

To prepare for this new challenge in 1953/54, we spent a fortnight under canvas at a campsite near Weston-super-Mare. The camp meant that we were all in great shape, and for me the camp was a great success because I managed to secure a place at inside left in the starting line-up for the opening games. At the end of August we played Derby County on a very boggy Eastville pitch and showed both our good form and excellent fitness by winning the contest 3-0. In fact, the winning margin could have been greater because we missed a penalty, another ball cannoned into the upright with the Derby keeper beaten and, in the closing ten minutes, we forced seven corners as the visitors wilted and our superior fitness shone through. Torrential overnight rain had saturated the pitch, so we decided to adopt simple tactics by pumping long balls down the middle and then giving chase. Our opponents did not adapt so well to the damp surface, and throughout the first half they persisted in playing short balls, most of which never found their destination. But even so, over half an hour had passed and the score was still standing at 0-0, when a long ball came down the right and I gathered it just outside the box. I quickly looked up and saw Ray Middleton, the Rams goalkeeper, running out towards me. I then lobbed the ball over his head and the deadlock was broken.

My calmness and vision were praised after the game in the newspapers, and I was lucky enough to maintain my goalscoring record in our next few games as I formed a useful striking partnership with Geoff Bradford. Geoff was the first Rovers player to be chosen for England while with the Bristol club – in fact, he's still the only Rovers player to have achieved this feat while at Eastville. Geoff was a superb centre-forward and could shoot equally well with both feet. He was so good that I gather Liverpool once made an offer in the region of £20,000 for him, but Bert, in this era of 'no buy, no sell', simply said no.

George Petherbridge was a fine player out wide, beating the opposition with his deceptive swerve and pace. Peter Hooper also made things difficult on the other side for defenders. Peter could also kick the ball with great power – in fact, in one match against Leicester, he took a penalty that hit the post and the ball rebounded back into our own half. From the breakaway, Leicester scored!

My own efforts drew the attention of the England selectors who were picking an England 'A' team. Apparently, one of the selectors contacted Bert Tann to enquire about my form, but Bert's reply was not that complimentary, so I was not chosen in the squad.

For the next few seasons, I continued to yo-yo between the Rovers' first team and their reserve side, but I managed to secure a decent run in the firsts after hitting a purple patch of goalscoring. In all, I scored 20 goals in my 40 League appearances during 1955/56, with only Geoff Bradford – with 25 in 26 appearances – scoring more. My good run of form included a match on Bonfire Night in November 1955, where I provided a few fireworks of my own by scoring a hat-trick as we beat Fulham 5-3 in an entertaining game. Their line-up was quite a strong one as well, with the likes of Bobby Robson, Jimmy Hill and the great Johnny Haynes, with whom I shared a round of golf in Durban when he finished his career in South Africa.

What they said about B.J.

John Atyeo – Bristol City and England footballer

Most men had to decide on one as the major sport and then play the other as a sideline – this is what happened in Barrie's case, but he was so talented at both that he was able to easily switch from cricket being his sideline to football being his second string.

I was privileged to play with him on several occasions – I found him to be reliable, hard-working and stylish, but never flashy. He always had a jovial and pleasant disposition, making him admirably suited to play team games, because of his ability to integrate so easily with his teammates and earn respect from his opponents.

Bert Tann – Coach and Manager, Bristol Rovers FC

Not long out of school, Barrie soon showed us that he was blessed with natural skill. Having only about a year before become the club coach, I was gratified that I had such potential to work with and, as was my habit in all such cases, I did what I could to encourage his skill.

His progress was good as he continued to develop his skills of control, accuracy of pass and the deceptive body swerve that allowed Barrie to establish himself among the best of Bristol's pure footballers.

He was cursed though with an inexplicable inconsistency that almost used to leave me in despair. By virtue of his own efforts or his good sense of position, he got into more good goal-scoring positions than most other players, but his ratio of goals to chances was not high and this, I believe, prevented Barrie going right to the very top in soccer.

BEATING MANCHESTER UNITED

My proudest moment in professional football came on 7 January 1956 when I was a member of the Rovers side that beat the mighty Manchester United at Eastville in the third round of the FA Cup. It was the greatest day in the club's history, and I was delighted to play a role in the famous victory and to get on the scoresheet as well.

At the time Manchester United were leading the First Division and, under Matt Busby, they had tasted much success in the years after the Second World War. They had won the FA Cup in 1948 and had been winners of the First Division in 1952, as well as being runners-up for three successive seasons between 1947 and 1949. They had at their disposal some outstanding young players – dubbed the 'Busby Babes' – and it was no surprise that the match programme for this cup tie, which I still proudly cherish, said, 'Manchester United can be regarded as the most successful and consistent club in post-war football. Eastville could not welcome a more attractive side, and there is scope for much good football from both sides.'

The match-day programme for the Rovers' most famous encounter.

We were in decent form ourselves in the Second Division of the Football League, lying in sixth place, level on points with Bristol City and just a couple of points behind leaders Sheffield Wednesday. The reserve side were also doing well in the Football Combination, lying in second place behind Tottenham Hotspur after winning 16 of their 23 games. Ron Nicholls, our second-choice keeper, was in the team for the cup match. Ron – with whom I subsequently played for so many years with Gloucestershire – had only made his League debut the previous weekend following an injury to our regular keeper Howard Radford, and the game against Manchester United was Ron's first ever FA Cup appearance.

The build-up to the match was something I had never experienced, and in fact I never saw anything like it again in my time as a footballer. When

---

| BR 55/56 — 182 |

F.A. CUP—3rd ROUND.   Kick-off 2.15 p.m.

BRISTOL ROVERS v. MANCHESTER UNITED
SATURDAY, JANUARY 7th, 1956.

Welcome—United

Manchester United can be regarded as the most successful and consistent club in post-war football. **They won the Cup in 1948, while in the First Division they were champions in 1952 and runners-up three seasons in succession between 1947 and 1949, while they were again second in 1951.**

They are the present leaders of the League and it may be said that **they run five teams all of which are at the head of their various competitions.** No wonder, Matt Busby, who was a model of a wing half in his playing days with Manchester City and Liverpool, is regarded as the foremost manager of the day.

ALL HAVE BEEN REPLACED

The Busby plan is to have replacements ready for the day when any of his players either depart or lose their form and, in this, he has succeeded admirably.

So much so, that he has had the satisfaction of seeing his entire defence chosen by England.

They are Ray Wood, the young goalkeeper, who hails from Hebburn on Tyne and who was signed from Darlington in 1949 at a fee of £5,000. He was in the Young England team against Italy two years ago and played for England against Wales and Ireland last season.

"Billy" Foulkes, the right back, cost the club only the usual £10 signing on fee. He is a native of St. Helen's and was in the England team against Ireland last season.

USEFUL DUNCAN EDWARDS

For the half back line, United have such players as Duncan Edwards, Jeff Whitefoot, Eddie Colman and Mark Jones.

Duncan Edwards became the first player during the past 50 years to be capped by England when only 18 and he played against Scotland last season. A Staffordshire lad, he captained England Boys as recently as the 1951-52 season and is equally at home in attack as in the middle line.

DUNCAN EDWARDS

Above: The editor's notes in the match-day programme.

Opposite: How the teams lined up.

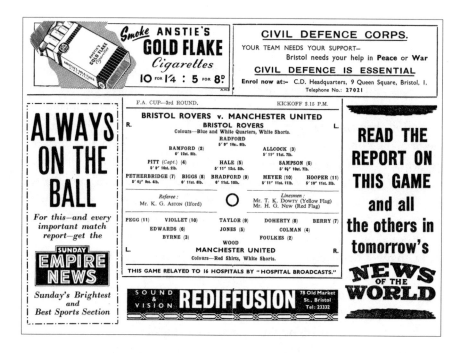

tickets for the tie first went on sale, there were queues of thousands of people outside the ground and, in and around Bristol in the fortnight or so before the game, talk about the cup tie overshadowed preparations for Christmas.

On the morning of the match, the streets around Eastville were soon awash with people, and the green buses of the Bristol Omnibus Company had to carefully weave their way in between as they carried even more people to the stadium. The Rovers' official record states that the crowd was 35,872, but there were probably another couple of thousand on top of that. There were quite a few people who were lucky enough to get complimentary tickets, including the drivers and conductors of the many buses that were parked up at the Muller Road End. There were also tens of thousands of people swarming around outside the ground, eager just to catch a glimpse of the 'Busby Babes'.

There were a few butterflies in my stomach as I got changed for the game, and several of my colleagues were feeling a bit nervous as well. But not our manager, Bert Tann, who came into the dressing room and gave us a stirring chat. In fact, I can still remember Bert's final words: 'Listen lads. Don't worry about that lot. We have eleven players, they have eleven. They are just another team. Now go out there and enjoy yourselves.'

As we trotted out onto the pitch behind our captain, Alfie Biggs, we were greeted with a huge roar. Apparently it could be heard for miles around and, like all my colleagues, it made the hairs on the back of my neck stand up. It was a dry and quite blustery afternoon, but the days before the game had been damp, so the pitch was quite muddy in places, with a liberal sprinkling of sand in the middle as well. This sea of mud was certainly a contributory factor behind our victory, as United normally played on good, true surfaces, but, equally as important, things went our way early on. Both teams were playing a 2-3-5 line-up, with two full-backs in defence, two wing halves plus a centre half in midfield, and a forward line comprising two wingers, two inside forwards and a centre forward. Peter Sampson and Geoff Bradford alongside me up front were soon into their stride, as we created early chances that tested Ray Wood, the United keeper. There was early action too for Ron Nicholls in our goal, as he dived well to save a waist-high shot from Roger Byrne, the United captain.

This was followed by a series of attacks on the United goal, with Geoff Bradford having another couple of good shots at goal after some good work out on the wing by George Petherbridge. The visitors then came back at us and created a good opening, but Dennis Viollet, despite being unmarked, headed the ball wide of the goal.

It had been quite a frenetic first twenty minutes and the scoreline was still 0-0, but the deadlock was broken when I managed to create an opening in midfield and then got a centre into the United goalmouth. The ball then cannoned off one of their defenders straight to Alfie Biggs, who deftly curled the ball into the net with his right foot, and another deafening roar went around the ground. A bit later, Alfie got a second chance to score, but his overhead shot just went over the bar. We also got a couple of free-kicks near the United box after the referee, Ken Aston, penalised the United defence for bringing down George Petherbridge. There were also some free-kicks at our end, including an indirect one taken by Roger Byrne from just outside the penalty area. He gave the ball an almighty wallop, hoping to get a deflection from the wall of players, but the ball instead whizzed high over the defenders and towards the far corner of the net. Ron Nicholls dived full length and just got the faintest of fingertips to the ball, but he couldn't stop the ball from ending up in the back of the net. The referee, not having seen Ron's little deflection, duly signalled for a goal kick instead of a goal.

We quickly rallied in the minutes before half-time with Alfie Biggs having a good header kicked off the goal line by Roger Byrne, while Geoff Bradford struck one into the side netting. We were into the final minute before the break. Frank Allcock played the ball to Geoff Bradford, who passed it out to George Petherbridge, who had another great run down the wing. His looping cross into the goalmouth came straight to me and, after quickly getting the ball under control, I had a shot that was blocked. But the ball bobbled back to me, and my second attempt went into the net to make it 2-0.

We got another huge cheer as we ran off with our lead and, after a few more stirring words from Bert Tann, we were determined not to let it slip. We soon went onto the attack in the second half, and forced Wood into making some more fine stops. Jack Pitt also sent a volley wide of the goal, while I had another shot at goal blocked by the United defence. But, after ten minutes or so, Alfie Biggs scored his second goal with a low strike from another fine cross from Geoff Bradford. In fact, 'The Baron', might have got his hat-trick shortly afterwards as he beat two defenders and then struck a scorching shot from about twenty yards out that Wood just managed to deflect over the bar. I also had a shot cleared off the line, but we went 4-0 up after Byrne had, in desperation, used his hands to stop a header from Geoff Bradford going into the net. Geoff duly took the penalty to send the crowd into a state of delirium as the score 4-0 went up on the board.

It was so emotional at the end as the referee's whistle blew. The huge crowd gave us a standing ovation – nobody tried to run onto the pitch, as in today's big sporting events, so we shook hands with the United team and hugged each other before gleefully making our way back to the changing rooms. The game was played in a fine spirit and, afterwards, as we were joyously celebrating in our communal bath, Matt Busby came in to compliment us on a tremendous victory. The better side had won, he said, and although his boys were disappointed at their losing they nevertheless recognised the skill and determination that our side had shown.

I felt ten feet tall the day after our victory, and it was great to read the accounts of our famous win in the evening and Sunday newspapers. The correspondent of the *Sunday Express* wrote how, 'Manchester United, leaders of the First Division, reeled off the pitch at Bristol yesterday after one of the worst drubbings in their history. Seldom have I seen a top-quality side so disorganised and demoralised.' In the *Daily Telegraph*, their reporter called it 'a magnificently balanced and executed victory, Manchester United were outclassed', while Desmond Hackett, the legendary football writer for the *Daily Express*, summed things up by saying that 'Bristol Rovers were the £110 team with the million-dollar touch of class'.

It was such a terrible shock in 1958 to hear about the awful Munich Air Disaster when so many of the Manchester United party lost their lives after a European Cup tie. I felt numb for hours after hearing the tragic news, and my mind immediately went back to the sporting way that the United players had taken our 4-0 victory over them. The football world lost some very skilful players, as well as some great ambassadors for the game that snowy night in Munich.

In my early years on the staff at Bristol Rovers, there was a break of ten weeks or so over the summer months in between the football seasons. Like me, several of the Rovers squad were decent cricketers and, after the hurly-burly of the football field, and the cold winter wind and rain, it was nice to play some sport in the sun. I had joined Stapleton Cricket Club as a batsman, and I managed to score a few runs for their side. It was commonplace at the time for some of the Rovers footballers to help out at Gloucestershire's County Ground, so Cecil Steeds, George Petherbridge and myself accepted an offer to work at the Nevil Road ground and, instead of kicking our heels during the weekdays, we helped out with odd jobs such as painting, selling scorecards and setting up the nets for the professional cricketers. We also got a chance to play in the nets as well, and with the county having a Club and Ground team, we also got the chance to play in a few of these games. I must have made a favourable impression because, when the Second XI were short for one of their games, I was invited to take part. I kept my place and, when the regular wicketkeeper was injured later in the season, 'Sonny' Avery, the county coach, had a chat with me about taking over. I had only kept before in the knockabout games with the Army, and had never had any formal coaching but, after one season with the seconds, Gloucestershire invited me to join their staff as a batsman and occasional wicketkeeper.

It didn't take me long to accept their offer, although my reasoning was not entirely based on cricketing reasons. Gloucestershire already had other specialist keepers on their staff, so I viewed the £5 per week as a rather nice way of keeping going in between the football seasons. Sonny Avery thought differently and believed that I was quite a talented player. He didn't like the way I treated the cricket as just a 'fill in' before the start of the next football season, and he made it quite clear that he would not waste his time with me unless my attitude was always positive and focused on the highest standards. Deep down I was actually enjoying the cricket, so I listened carefully to Sonny's advice and vowed to work hard at my game. As it turned out, his advice changed my whole sporting life.

FOUR

My Career with Gloucestershire

Between 1936 and the mid-1950s Andy Wilson had been Gloucestershire's wicketkeeper. He was a very fine keeper and had played alongside some of the great names in the county's history – such as Wally Hammond and Charlie Barnett – and he had kept wicket to a legion of top-class bowlers, including Tom Goddard, 'Bomber' Wells and Sam Cook. A man of such vast experience and talent was clearly worth watching so, while at the County Ground, I took every opportunity to watch Andy in action. Even when doing a few odd jobs around the ground, I would ensure that I got into a good vantage point to pick up a few tricks of the trade if Gloucestershire were in the field.

My first full year on the staff proved to be Andy's last and, for much of the summer, it was Yorkshire-born Peter Rochford who was behind the stumps. Peter had made his Championship debut for Gloucestershire in 1952 and, in 1954, he had started to play on a more regular basis as the many years of wear and tear on the county circuit took their toll on Andy. Like Andy, Peter was a very fine wicketkeeper with razor-sharp reflexes and the softest of hands. He would make keeping wicket to the spinners on the dusty wickets at Bristol look the easiest job in the world, and some people, I gather, felt that he was good enough to be a reserve wicketkeeper on an MCC winter tour abroad. Yet, despite being a brilliant man behind the stumps, Peter ruffled more than a few feathers and he fell out with the county's authorities. Although he usually wore a neat and dapper lounge suit, Peter did not readily conform, and he hated some of the restrictions imposed from on-high, especially as far as what happened after play was concerned. He could be a real charmer and amusing company, but he also liked a drink, and was not afraid to speak his mind. He was less intimidated by the senior professionals than some others on the county's books, and there were times when Peter had a few verbal spats with the older players.

At first, the club officials turned a blind eye to Peter's indiscretions or drinking excesses, probably in the hope that he would settle down and toe the line. But his brushes with the authorities continued and, in 1957, I got my first taste of County Championship cricket. I'd been in decent form with both the gloves and the bat for the seconds and also in club cricket in the Bristol Leagues. With Peter struggling with illness as well as being out of form with the bat and out of favour as well, I was called up into the Gloucestershire side for the match against Essex at Gidea Park in Romford at the end of May 1957.

My first victim was Mickey Bear, who I caught off 'Bomber' Wells. I didn't concede any byes and, at number seven in the order, I made 18 and 30 without being dismissed in either innings. I can still remember the words of Brian 'Tonker' Taylor, the great Essex wicketkeeper, when I walked out to the wicket and took guard for the first time. 'Tonker' was standing up behind the stumps to Ian King, and he quietly told me to take my time taking guard and to prepare properly. Fortunately I got a thick edge onto my first delivery and it flew past Tonker's gloves for a couple of runs. As I ran back down the wicket to complete the second run, 'Tonker' turned to me and said, 'Well done, Barrie. You're off the mark, but from now on, you are on your own!' Of course, getting one off the mark doesn't happen any longer, but that was how the game was played then.

Overall, I had a decent game and, as a result, I kept my place until the end of June when Bobby Etheridge was given a run behind the stumps for the next dozen Championship matches. Peter Rochford returned to the side in mid-August as Gloucestershire headed to Cheltenham for the annual festival. He appeared in the first two games of the festival, with Gloucestershire winning the second against Hampshire by 6 wickets. But he was then replaced by Etheridge for the next match against Yorkshire, which was Sam Cook's Benefit match. It turned out to be a closely fought encounter and, in a tense run-chase, Bobby settled the issue with a huge six.

By this time I was back to Eastville undertaking pre-season training, but I kept a close link with the Gloucestershire team, and soon heard that Peter had not been offered a new contract by the county. With Bobby Etheridge also on footballing duty with Bristol City, Ron Nicholls had kept wicket for Gloucestershire in their last three Championship matches of the summer.

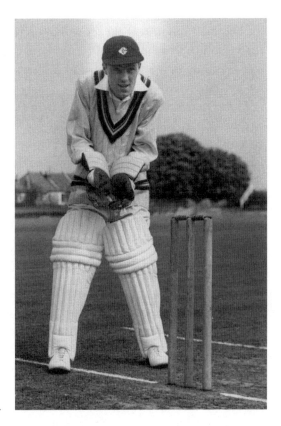

B.J. in April 1957.

Having started the 1957 cricket season very much as one of the lesser lights of the Gloucestershire squad, I had finished it as the reserve to Bobby Etheridge. I was perfectly happy with this arrangement, as football was still my main love, and I had quite a reasonable season with Bristol Rovers in 1957/58, starting the season in good form with a hat-trick against Derby County as we defeated the Rams 5-2.

But things started to change in the spring of 1958 as Bobby decided to go off on Bristol City's end-of-season tour of Germany. I was left as the only wicketkeeper on the county's books for the first few games of the season. 'You are going to have to play,' George Emmett, the Gloucestershire captain, told me, adding, 'but I will play you for the first six games to see how you get on, and then when Bobby returns, we'll see how things are.' I duly played in these games and, when Bobby came back, Emmett took me aside and said, 'We think that you have done very well, Barrie, so we'll give you another six games as well.' This came as a bit of a surprise to me because I had never held any ambitions to play professional cricket. I was really a footballer filling in, but clearly I was doing something right and then, halfway through the season, against Sussex at Bristol, came another shock, when George presented me with my county cap. I was flabbergasted!

There were several other footballers in the Gloucestershire side, such as Arthur Milton, who had played League football for Arsenal and Bristol City and, unlike me, was good enough to play both cricket and football at international level. Nobody since has achieved that feat for England and I don't think anybody ever will because nowadays there just isn't that sort of space during the seasons, and the players are well enough paid just to be able to concentrate on one sport. I had been fortunate enough to see Arthur play in his only soccer international at Wembley – he was a magnificent footballer and a gifted cricketer as well. He excelled close to the wicket as a fielder, and was a free-scoring batsman who could have played in more than 6 Tests for England had he not been affected by injury, breaking his hand in a Test in Australia on the 1958/59 tour and having to be flown home.

Ron Nicholls, the county's middle-order batsman, also kept goal at various times for Bristol Rovers, Cardiff City, Bristol City and Cheltenham Town. I was delighted to see Ron record his maiden Championship hundred in 1958 defying Surrey – the reigning County Champions – for over four-and-a-half hours with a display of fierce pulls and cuts, as well as many sweetly timed drives on the off-side and deft glances off his legs. Had it not rained on the final day of this match at Bristol, Ron's efforts might have helped us win the game.

During that season, Ron scored 919 runs in Championship, while Tom Graveney, his partner at number four in the order, amassed 1,106 runs against county opposition. Tom missed a few games with us because of his Test commitments with England, and also injury but, when he was available, he was a fine sight in full flow, and his cultured stroke-play lit up many a grey and cloudy day at the Nevil Road ground.

Our leading run-scorer during 1958 was opening batsman Martin Young. In all, Martin scored 1,755 runs in the Championship that year, with five centuries to his name. On the field he was an assertive figure, while off it he cut a sophisticated figure with his immaculate dress sense, and was very much the gentleman cricketer. He had briefly played for Worcestershire before joining Gloucestershire in 1949 and developing into a steady opening batsman with a solid technique. He also had a few quirky mannerisms as well, such as kissing his bat before walking out to the wicket.

The spearhead of our bowling attack in 1958 was our spin partnership of John Mortimore and Sam Cook. They each bowled over 900 overs in the Championship, with John claiming 84 wickets in the competition, and Sam exactly 100. John was a fine spinner with the classical off-spinner's delivery that turned into the right-handers, as well as a clever variation with one that floated past the outside edge. John was not the biggest spinner of a ball that I ever kept to, but he was perhaps one of the most accurate, and his exceptional powers of putting the ball roughly in the same place over after over and tying down the batsmen made for some cat-and-mouse cricket, and I always enjoyed the way he carefully and patiently plotted a batsman's downfall. After his success in 1958, and a couple of seasons before that, I was not the least bit surprised to hear later in November that John had been given the call to fly out to Australia to reinforce the MCC party.

Sam was the senior spinner and had given honest and loyal service to Gloucestershire since the 1946 season when he had arrived, virtually unknown, and had impressed the great Wally Hammond with his left-arm spin. Like John, he also possessed an immaculate length and skilful flight, but Sam had a much lower trajectory than the taller off-spinner. He had, though, just as many cunning variations, and it was fascinating to see him pit his wits against opposition batsmen, often deceiving them into playing and missing, and then looking down the wicket at them with a wicked smile on his face.

As far as results were concerned, 1958 was a disappointing first summer for me in the Gloucestershire side. In all we won just 5 out of our 28 Championship matches that season, with only Glamorgan, Warwickshire and Nottinghamshire below us in the table, as we rued our bad luck with the weather plus a few injuries as well. Two of our wins came in the final couple of matches of the summer – against Lancashire and Leicestershire – with the former being our captain George Emmett's final game at Bristol before retiring from first-class cricket to become the captain of our Second XI. George marked what had been intended as his final match at the County Ground with a memorable hundred – his only one of that summer – and as he walked off he got a standing ovation from the decent-sized and appreciative crowd, plus all of the opposition as well. He truly deserved it as well, having been one of the mainstays of the Gloucestershire side since 1936, and during his career having hit over 22,000 first-class runs.

I only saw George quite late in his career, but I was immediately impressed by his elegant and fluent stroke-play, plus his assertive approach to batting, even in the most dire situations. Despite his slight frame, George could unleash some powerful strokes and, as a youngster on Gloucestershire's staff, I could not fathom how a player of his obvious class had only played a single Test for England. George's new role in 1959 was to help groom the emerging talent in our Second XI, but another crop of injuries in our batting line-up saw him return to first-team action. It was nearly a fairytale return as well, as we made an exciting bid for the county title.

Tom Graveney had taken over from George as First XI captain, but a nasty finger injury meant that Tom spent much of the summer on the sidelines, and George was recalled to share the captain's duties with Arthur Milton. In mid-May we recorded our first Championship win of the summer, beating Somerset at Taunton by 4 wickets, before travelling up to Derby where we won again – this time by 48 runs as our spinners Sam Cook and John Mortimore, plus paceman Tony Brown, bowled us to victory.

The trio played a decisive role in our innings victory over Leicestershire in early June at Bristol. The visitors were shot out for just 80 in their second innings, with the two spinners in particular preying on some uncertain batting. Sam took 3 for 19 in 13 overs, while John had the remarkable figures of 12.5-9-7-5. Our next Championship match at Bristol saw another innings victory as we completed the double over Derbyshire and, by mid-summer, with us riding high in the Championship table, there was plenty of talk around the Nevil Road ground and in the local papers about a first county title coming to Gloucestershire.

It was quite satisfying for me as well to read several very complimentary articles about my wicketkeeping. I was really enjoying my new job with the gloves, and my batting was developing quite nicely too. As a result of my steadiness, I was promoted up to number three for a couple of matches, and was quite happy to be asked to be nightwatchman at other times. I also got the opportunity to play a couple of quite decisive innings during our run chases – the first came in our match in July against Northamptonshire at Bristol. A fine spell of off-spin by young David Allen had allowed us to dismiss the visitors on the first day for 142, but then their pace bowler Frank Tyson struck back and took 6 for 29, including myself for 12, as they secured a small first-innings lead. As the game progressed, the wicket started to turn quite sharply and, on the final day, we chased the quite stiff target of 193 in four-and-a-half hours. Martin Young then played a magnificent innings, fending off Tyson's pace, and then getting the score-board moving against the spinners. But, as the ball became older, the spinners worked their way through our batting and, when I walked to the wicket, we were still 32 runs away from the target with only 2 wickets left, and just Sam Cook left in the pavilion, whose career batting average was only 5.

I had a quick chat with Martin and told him that I would try and drop anchor so that he could continue to work the ball around with-out taking too many risks. Our plan worked well for a while, and we were within 6 runs of our target when Martin, having just reached a most well-deserved century, skied the ball towards deep fine-leg. My heart was in my mouth as we thought about a run but, to our delight, Jack Manning spilled the chance and we saw Gloucestershire home, with Martin walking off with a fine 108 to his name, and myself unbeaten on 2.

In early August I was involved in a second and even more dramatic run-chase as we were set a tricky target of 212 in a fraction over two-and-three-quarter hours to beat Essex at Leyton. With Surrey, the County Champions, likely to lose at Worcester, and fellow challengers Yorkshire having already beaten Middlesex at Scarborough, we knew that we had to record another victory if we were going to maintain our bid for the county title. For a while it looked as if we had squandered our chances as we slumped to 131 for 8 and, with plenty of time remaining, I joined Tony Brown at the crease thinking that for the next hour or so I was going to have to stubbornly fend off the Essex bowlers if we were going to salvage a draw. But Tony had other ideas and, as I continued to play defensively, he went onto the attack, turning the game on its head with a fusillade of strokes. In all, he boldly struck 4 sixes and 10 fours as we brought up the 200, and brought the equation down to a handful of runs.

In a last throw of the dice, Doug Insole, the Essex captain, decided to take the new ball and recall his pace bowlers. His plan looked to have back-fired as Tony and I continued to gather a few runs, but then, with the score on 209 for 8, Tony was caught behind off Trevor Bailey. There was frantic excitement around the ground as Sam Cook trudged to the wicket with 3 runs still needed. Trevor Bailey then bowled a wide and I was able to bring the scores level with a single. Sam had few pretensions as a batsman, but he looked to have struck the winning runs as he flicked a delivery from Bailey off his legs, but Joe Milner at short-leg stuck out his left hand and took a fine catch to leave the match tied.

This thrilling game at Leyton had kept us in the title hunt, and the next day we started the first of three games at the Cheltenham Festival eager to maintain our challenge. But our fielding let us down in the opening match as a century from Peter Walker helped Glamorgan secure a convincing innings win. We then returned to winning ways when we beat Middlesex by an innings, overcoming some inclement weather that had looked likely to frustrate us further after we had elected to bat first. As it turned out, the rain helped to spice up the wicket for our spinners, and Sam and John took 17 wickets between them as we completed an important victory shortly before lunch on the third day.

That night Martin and several others went out on the town to celebrate. Unfortunately, Martin later had a big argument with a tree in the middle of the High Street – he claimed, of course, that the tree hadn't been there the day before! Anyhow, he was still feeling a little bit tired and shaken up the next morning as we gathered at the College Ground on the Saturday morning for the start of the next match of the festival, against the Indian tourists. With Martin still not 100 per cent, George Emmett asked me if I would be prepared to have a go as an opening batsman. Even though I usually batted at number nine, I said yes, and then had another surprise when, after winning the toss, Pankaj Roy, the Indian captain, asked us to bat first. We were not going to turn down the opportunity of taking first use of the wicket, especially as the side batting first on the college wicket usually had a distinct advantage.

My partner was Arthur Milton, and we added 124 in around two-and-a-half hours before I was run out for 63 – a score that remained as my highest ever for the county. I did get a few more chances over the years to go in up the order, and I did in fact make 63 twice more, against Oxford University in 1962 and Sussex in 1964. It had been a great thrill to reach fifty and to raise my bat in appreciation of the applause from the large crowd and the inhabitants of the many gaily coloured marquees that ringed the boundary. They had plenty to cheer about later in our innings as George Emmett came in and, in the space of an hour and a quarter, he struck a quite brilliant 85. Then, on the final morning, George set the tourists a target of 326 in a shade under five hours, but some fine seam bowling from David Smith, supported by some typically accurate off-spin from John Mortimore, saw India being bowled out for 133. This victory by 192 runs gave a further boost to our morale as we entered the final part of the season still in with a shout of winning the county title. Our hopes were given another lift by a win inside two days over Kent at Dover, and we returned to the West Country knowing that our next two matches – against Yorkshire at Bristol and Surrey at Gloucester – would probably decide the outcome of the title.

Fortunately, Tom Graveney was fit enough to play a decisive innings against Yorkshire, and he helped us overcome a shaky start against the Yorkshire new-ball attack. He drove with authority to make 67, and then John Mortimore displayed his all-round skills with an aggressive 76. David Smith and I added 71 for the ninth wicket before we declared on 294 for 8. Tony Brown then produced one of the most remarkable displays of seam bowling, taking 7 for 11 from 65 deliveries as Yorkshire were bustled out for 35 and we gleefully took the field again as the Tykes followed on. They were, admittedly, without several of their Test players, but even so it only took an hour on the final morning to wrap up a decisive victory over one of our fellow title seekers.

Our next match, on Gloucester's Wagonworks ground, saw our three slow bowlers – Sam Cook, David Allen and John Mortimore – up against Surrey's fine spinners Jim Laker and Tony Lock. Alec Bedser, the visiting captain, won the all-important toss, but it was first blood to Gloucestershire as, in the space of three-and-a-half hours, our spin trio had dismissed Surrey for just 130. After just three overs of seam at the start of our innings, Lock and Laker were straight into action, and they soon found the Gloucester wicket to their liking as we were bustled out for 101. Tom Graveney made 31 before being caught and bowled by Lock, and I was second top-scorer with 17 towards the end as Surrey gained a decisive lead of 29. When Surrey batted again, Sam Cook struck with his first two deliveries, but Ken Barrington then counterattacked. I later got to know Kenny quite well when England were touring South Africa in 1964/65, and we often reminisced about this match and the way his first scoring shot was to hoist Sam for an enormous six into the crowd. Sam later got his revenge having Kenny caught by Arthur Milton but, by this time, he had 49 runs to his name, and Surrey had gained a lead of over a hundred.

We ended up needing 161 and, with the wicket having become a spinner's paradise, Bedser opened up immediately with Lock and Laker. They immediately got the ball to lift and turn alarmingly and we slumped to 26 for 7 before the two Davids – Allen and Smith – briefly offered some resistance to show that run-scoring was possible. But, with the ball spinning and also rising up, it was only a matter of time before our innings ended, and we were duly dismissed for 71. Surrey had won by 89 runs, and with the match went our aspirations of winning the County Championship. But we were then given a lifeline as Surrey drew with Middlesex, and we travelled to Worcester for our final match of the summer knowing that we still had a chance, albeit a very slim one, of winning the title if we could take 14 points from the match. But, by the close of the first day's play, our faint hopes had completely evaporated as, after dismissing Worcestershire for 205, we slipped to 38 for 6 against the home team's lively new-ball attack. We duly ended up 94 runs in arrears and, on the last day, were set a stiff challenge of making 362. Martin Young tried his best with a typically accomplished century, but we lost wickets at regular intervals and eventually fell 84 runs short of the target.

As we headed home to Bristol, news came through from Hove where Yorkshire were playing Sussex that the Tykes had won an exciting run-chase. They had successfully made 215 in 105 minutes with 5 wickets in hand, and it was Yorkshire who ended Surrey's long reign of seven years as County Champions. Gloucestershire were the runners-up, and I headed back to football training with Bristol Rovers hoping that I might one day get another chance of being in a Championship-winning team. Sadly, it was not to be.

What they said about B.J.

Jim Parks – Sussex and England wicketkeeper

Keepers come in all types. Some flashy, some sedate, many noisy, a few silent. For Barrie, there was never the need for showmanship. His work behind the stumps was done with the quiet efficiency of a man who knows what true professionalism is all about. With two top-class off-spinners regularly in action, most of Barrie's work was difficult and the notorious dust of the Bristol wicket made his life even more hazardous.

Although it was as one of the country's foremost wicketkeepers that Barrie made his name, he also performed some sterling work in front of the stumps, batting during his career anywhere from one to eleven, and he was the type of player the opposition were always pleased to see walking back to the pavilion.

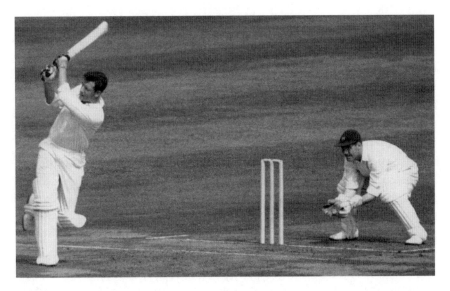

Bob Gale pulls a ball from David Allen in the Championship match between Middlesex and Gloucestershire in September 1961.

TOM GRAVENEY AND THE GLORIOUS GLOSTERS

Without doubt, Tom Graveney was the finest batsman in our side in the late 1950s. In fact, he was one of England's finest county batsmen of the 1950s, and it did not take me long to appreciate what a superb craftsman he was. We were playing against Warwickshire at Edgbaston, and I had joined Tom at the crease after we had lost several wickets. At the time, he was on 88, and he strolled down the wicket to ask me if I had faced a leg-spinner before. I replied that I hadn't, to which he replied, 'Well, just see off the remaining 3 balls of this over, and don't do anything silly.' The bowler in question was Eric Hollies, the great England leg-spinner and, as a result of good fortune rather than great skill, I just about managed to survive the 3 balls. Tom then took over and calmly monopolised the strike, reaching his hundred without any more alarms in no time at all. It was a great education for me at the other end and, curiously, exactly the same thing happened second time around. He was approaching his hundred when I came in to bat against the spinners. After I had narrowly survived again, Tom then reached his second century of the game.

Tom Graveney was a truly magnificent player and, to my mind, the most stylish batsman that we ever had in my time at Gloucestershire. In 1959 Tom took over the job, but during the season there were some club officials who felt that the captaincy was affecting his batting. During the summer a gentleman called Tom Pugh was introduced into the Gloucestershire side. He had been recommended to us by a gentleman in London, but Tom had no background at all as far as first-class cricket was concerned, and as far as we could tell had only been playing club cricket. He was a very nice bloke but, as far as his playing credentials were concerned, he was limited in his stroke making, and we felt his inexperience and lack of technique were insufficient for the county game. Nevertheless, Tom Pugh played a few matches for us in 1959, and then again in 1960, when Tom Graveney was still the appointed captain. We did not though have a particularly good season and, given the potential we had, we were underachieving. But then came the news during the winter that Tom Pugh had been appointed captain for 1961. The manner in which this was done was poor, as Tom Graveney had not been told face-to-face that he was being replaced as captain and had read of Tom Pugh's appointment in the newspapers. Not surprisingly, Tom Graveney was very upset, left Gloucestershire and moved to Worcestershire.

We soon heard the news about Tom Graveney's departure during the winter months and, before the season began, half a dozen or so of the senior capped players held a meeting and agreed that, although he was a very pleasant and determined fellow, it was unwise for Tom Pugh to take over as the county's captain. He was approached by us and told that we didn't think that he was the right man for the job. But he disagreed and said that, as he had been appointed by the county, he had decided to carry out his duties as captain.

It was against this background that we started the 1961 season, with matches at Oxford University, and then at Bristol against Leicestershire and Warwickshire, before playing the MCC at Lord's and Northamptonshire at Peterborough. By the time we left Lord's for the match in Northants, it had become obvious to the senior players in the Gloucestershire camp that Tom's captaincy left a lot to be desired. He was very determined and, although we had won the games, we had not exactly shone as a well-led XI in these matches, where the victories had come about as a result of things other than inspired captaincy.

A rather embarrassing incident then took place at Peterborough, concerning the new ball. The common practice was for a yellow disc to be placed adjacent to the scoreboard after 80 overs had been bowled, indicating that the new ball was due in 5 overs and then, after 85 had been bowled, a second white disc would be added. This duly happened when we were in the field as Northants batted first at Peterborough, with the discs placed alongside the scorer's tent, which was one of many tents and marquees around the edge of the pretty ground. But Tom did not call for the new ball and, after 3 overs had elapsed, with David Smith and Tony Brown champing at the bit, he still showed no reaction to the discs going up. By now David Smith had lost patience and confronted Tom, asking him why he was not asking for the new ball. His reply was that it was not due yet, as the discs had not gone up, and as he said this he pointed over to the opposite side of the ground to a tent that was selling ice cream. David then had to redirect Tom's attention back to the tent in which the scorers were sitting! Although hilarious, it was quite embarrassing for Tom, but there was still more to come that day. After Northants were eventually dismissed for 295, David Larter, their tall quick bowler, built up quite a head of steam and when poor old Tom went in to bat, he misjudged a delivery from Larter, and ducked into a full toss thinking that it was a bouncer. Not only did it break his jaw but, because he had ducked so low, he was also given out lbw by the umpire. All in all, not a very good day for our captain.

After we were dismissed for 216, Northants then went for quick runs and left us with a target of 304. With Arthur Milton now at the helm, we won the game by 4 wickets, and Arthur, by common consent from the rest of the team, retained the captaincy for the rest of the season.

The match at Peterborough had been a rather unfortunate and painful way for Tom Pugh to forego the captaincy. One of the best things that Tom did for us was to arrange a pre-season tour to Bermuda. The visit in early April, though, began with four of us – David Carpenter, Arthur Milton, Dennis A'Court and myself – contracting tonsillitis. You can imagine our frustration and dismay as we were told to stay in our hotel rooms for the next five days, while the rest of the squad were out there enjoying themselves, keeping fit, having a couple of beers and meeting people.

The only advantage that came out of it was when we did recover and got back into the swing of things, the four of us hadn't spent any money, so the rest of the team were sidling up asking for us to help them out with expenses. We also got a chance to play in a couple of football matches, including one against the Bermudan national team. The great Stanley Matthews was coaching over there at the same time, and he made a guest appearance in our side against the Bermudans – it was a great thrill to play alongside him.

Another bonus came on our return flight back home, where one of the stewards turned out to be Ernie Palmer, an old mate of mine from National Service days. The Gloucestershire party therefore got preferential treatment with the liquor and special food coming out from the first-class section to us 'plebs' at the back!

The Gloucestershire side at the time had some very useful bowlers. At the time we were playing on uncovered wickets, which meant that, on several occasions, our bowlers were performing on damp surfaces. At Bristol, the ball was already renowned to keep low, so on these occasions it would skid through from the seam of David Smith and the swing of Tony Brown. My job became no easier when keeping on these wet wickets to the off-spin of David Allen and John Mortimore, or Sam Cook's left-arm spin. They made life difficult for me in any case because of the prodigious spin they extracted on the sandy wickets at Bristol. It became even more testing when the surface became damp, and the ball almost turned square.

Fortunately, we also had some good catchers close to the wicket, especially Tony Brown who, in one game at Trent Bridge, held onto a record six catches in an innings. It could have been seven, but when a big skier had gone up from one of the Nottinghamshire openers, I shouted for it, simply because I had the gloves on. Tony had also shouted out, but he then stood back and let me take the catch – I often wonder if I deprived him of an even greater record in the history books!

Tony was not averse either to the odd little joke on the field, such as the time we were playing Derbyshire at Derby. Derek Morgan, the home team's captain, was batting at the time, and I was standing up to one of the spinners as Derek flicked the ball off his legs to backward square leg and set off for a run. It looked like a long single and, as I turned around to get into position, I wasn't sure if Derek would try to look for a second. I had my back to the running batsmen as the ball was thrown back in from the deep, and then I heard Tony's voice loudly saying 'Quick, B.J.! Take 'em off!' I duly gathered in the ball, dived full length and knocked down all three stumps with a huge roar. But my glee quickly turned to embarrassment as I looked up to see Derek calmly sitting on his bat at the non-striker's end and, like everyone else, he was laughing his head off.

During the 1965 season, two teenage cricketers joined us from South Africa – Barry Richards and Mike Procter. Both were very promising, and had joined us because the previous winter, on the England tour to South Africa, David Allen had seen them in action, and had recommended that they should play a few second-team games with us. The only time that Barry and Mike could play together for the first team was when we were playing a touring team and, by a strange stroke of coincidence, the Springboks were the visitors to Bristol in mid-July. Sadly, heavy rain limited play to just the first day, but we soon saw their huge potential. Both made impressive half-centuries, with Barry making a composed 59 before being caught and bowled by Peter Pollock, and Mike scoring 69 before he was caught by Dennis Gamsy, the wicketkeeper, off Pollock.

We could see straight away that these two lads were potentially world-class cricketers, but we could only subsequently play one of them, as the regulations at the time would not allow us to play both. We duly kept hold of Mike, and he developed into one of the finest all-rounders of all time. I kept wicket to him when he was a young fast bowler, and he was very sharp with a deceptive action, bowling with a windmill action almost off the wrong foot. In fact, the mark that I made to stand back to him was a good four feet further back from where I would normally stand, and none of our other seam bowlers were slouches either. He did a tremendous amount of good work for the county, as well as creating a lot of goodwill off the field, by being a fine ambassador for the game. He became the mainstay of the side and was so instrumental in Gloucestershire winning a couple of one-day titles in the 1970s that the Press coined the name 'Proctershire' for the side!

What they said about B.J.

Tony Brown – captain of Gloucestershire 1969-1976

You will not find a more sincere or honest cricketer than Barrie – he was well-liked and trusted by everyone who knew him. On the cricket field, he did a wonderfully consistent job behind the stumps and on numerous occasions he was the man on the spot when a few runs were needed for victory and one mistake could mean defeat.

He rarely failed his team in such circumstances. I well remember a six back over the bowler's head against his native county Hampshire; a cover drive for four at Trent Bridge; a scampered single at Bristol; a hook for four at Peterborough – all shots to win games for us in the dying minutes with the pressure really on.

It is often said that the wicketkeeper is the hub of the play when the team is fielding – everything revolves around him. In Barrie's case this was also true off the field, as he was a wonderful team man. If anybody needed cheering up or had a problem, Barrie was always there to help. Nothing was too much trouble for him and, with his keen and friendly sense of humour, he was always the one to lift the veil off a gloomy situation. After over twenty years of playing soccer and cricket for a living, he knew all about the problems that can affect professional team games, yet he always was prepared to solve, rather than magnify the problems.

THE COUNTY CIRCUIT

Up until 1963 I was playing professional sport all year round without a break, alternating from football with Bristol Rovers to county cricket with Gloucestershire and then back to football again. I wasn't alone either, as Ron Nicholls also alternated between the games. We were both as happy as Larry, until Bert Tann, the Rovers manager gave us an ultimatum – we either played soccer and reported for pre-season training or he would put us on the transfer list and make us available to another club. As the end of the cricket season overlapped the pre-season training, we were forced into making a choice. We ended up though both deciding to stay with Gloucestershire until the end of September.

Bert took umbrage at this, and he immediately transfer-listed us, making both Ron and I available to another club provided a decent fee was paid. In addition, we lost our weekly wage of around £20 once the season started, but I wasn't too upset, because cricket had started to take over my life. In all honesty, I felt that my best years as a footballer were now behind me, and that I was likely to play for longer as a cricketer than as a footballer. Even so, I was still keen to play football in between the cricket seasons, and several clubs showed an interest in signing me, including Plymouth Argyle. As it turned out though, I had little choice – Bert had an interest in one of the Argyle players and I became part of the deal that saw me move to Plymouth in August 1958 for £4,500.

I duly had a season with the Plymouth club, scoring 5 goals in 8 League appearances before being transfer-listed again and being snapped up by Newport County. I was pleased to be returning to Severnside and I spent two-and-a-half years playing for the Newport side. In all, I made 70 League appearances for Newport County and scored 27 goals, as well as creating many others for my colleagues. Perhaps my most important goal for the Welsh club came in the second round of their FA Cup tie away to non-League Salisbury. It was quite a tricky tie for the League club, but my goal clinched a 1-0 victory and, perhaps more importantly, a very attractive home tie against Tottenham Hotspur. A capacity crowd of 24,000 were present at Somerton Park for the visit of Spurs' great players, and it was a pleasure to take the field against the likes of Danny Blanchflower, Dave Mackay, John White, Bobby Smith and Cliff Jones. I came close to scoring in the first half, which proved to be a close-fought affair, but in the end Tottenham's class told in the second half as they won 4-0.

I was transfer-listed again at the end of the 1960/61 season. Minehead, the Western League side, and Cheltenham Town from the Southern League, both quickly offered me terms, but I decided to wait, as I still felt I was good enough to play in the Football League rather than a non-League outfit. I was right as, in September 1961, I was approached by Bristol City, and they agreed to pay £850 for my transfer. I duly played in 11 matches for them, scoring 8 goals and, in my final ever League appearance, in April 1963, I recorded another hat-trick as we beat Southend United 6-3, with Bobby 'Shadow' Williams also netting three. Fred Ford, the Bristol City manager, had told me before I had signed that I would be cover for the first team, and I was only in the starting line-up against Southend because the regular player in my position, Brian Clark, was injured. Despite my scoring three goals, Brian resumed his place for the following game against Bristol Rovers and I returned to the reserves.

Not many players can boast a hat-trick on their final League appearance, and I was proud to have signed off in this way. However, by this time I was finding that keeping the two careers going was too demanding – both mentally and physically – so, in the spring of 1963, when the Bristol City management indicated that they would guarantee offering me a contract for the following winter, I knew that it was time to hang up my football boots and concentrate instead on cricket.

I was lucky to be in a Gloucestershire side that was full of great cricketers and all-round sportsmen. We really enjoyed ourselves travelling around the country, and I was very grateful that I was fit and strong enough to enjoy this second phase of my sporting career. During my cricket career, I saw many changes to the county game – over time, there was more and more one-day cricket, while the distinction between the amateurs and professionals was dispensed with in 1963.

Another difference was that, back in the early 1960s, many of the county games were played on quite poor wickets and often in bad weather conditions. Three examples stand out in my memory – the first when Gloucestershire entertained the 1960 South Africans at Bristol. The pitch at Nevil Road was, to say the least, up and down, and not really the kind of surface to expect the calibre of a touring side to play upon. The Springboks gained the advantage of batting first, and they mustered 116 before we were dismissed for 81, with all of our batsmen finding it difficult to play against the likes of Neil Adcock, 'Toey' Tayfield, Trevor Goddard and James Pothecary on the poor wicket. The tourists were then bowled out for 49, with Dennis A'Court bowling superbly to take 6 for 25 while, at the other end, David Smith took 4 for 20 in 12 overs to leave us needing 85 to win. Both sides were nonplussed about the way the ball was behaving, and we were not that confident as Martin Young and Tom Pugh went out to open the innings. It didn't take Adcock long to get cracking, as Pugh was caught behind for a duck before Derek Hawkins touched an outswinger, with the score on 17 for 2 at lunch.

After the interval, Martin Young and Tom Graveney helped to double the score, and our morale started to rise as the two batsmen grew in confidence. But, with the total on 36, Adcock bowled a viciously swinging ball that uprooted Young's leg stump and, not long after, Graveney went for 14. Adcock continued to trouble the new batsmen, but Ron Nicholls started to play some superb strokes, which gradually eased us towards our victory target. But wickets still fell at regular intervals and, by the time I arrived at the crease, we still needed 20 more runs with 3 wickets remaining. We decided that Ron should try and face Adcock as much as possible, with me blocking it out at the other end. The gameplan worked as Ron hit a few more boundaries and I made a magnificent 0, as we reached our victory target without losing any more wickets. There were several smiles around the ground because Gloucestershire had won but, in truth, it wasn't that exciting a game, because batting had become something of a lottery with the inconsistent bounce and very unpredictable wicket.

The groundsman at the County Ground at that time was Bernie Bloodworth – another real character! Bernie had played for Gloucestershire between 1919 and 1932 as their reserve keeper and an occasional left-arm spinner. After retiring from playing, Bernie initially became the county's scorer and baggage-man, in addition to being Wally Hammond's personal valet – a role he was swooningly proud to play, carefully laying out his flannels before a game and taking great care of his bats and other equipment. In addition to this role as general factotum, Bernie would also spend hours working away on the Nevil Road square, always wearing his trademark brown trilby. On non-match days, it was a common sight to see Bernie out in the middle for hours, rolling sand into the wicket and the surrounding areas. He was a genial soul, but if anyone questioned the quality of his wickets his riposte was always a swift and withering 'but Wally could bat on it!'

The second example of a match played in different conditions was against Glamorgan in August 1962 on the Steel Company of Wales' ground at Margam, adjacent to their large steelworks at Port Talbot. Throughout the game a foul-smelling cloud drifted across the pitch from the smelting works, but this was the least of our worries, as the entire ground was like a wet sponge. Whenever the ball was played into the outfield it just stopped, making runs almost impossible to make. Given the conditions it was no surprise that both first innings were completed on the first day – we made 88 to which Glamorgan replied with 62, and by 5.30 p.m. Martin Young and Ron Nicholls were back at the crease, making 38 without being separated before the umpires called time. Rain washed out the second day and, after an hour's delay, the contest resumed on the third day. From 38 for 0 we slumped to 92 all out, but this was enough to secure a win, as Glamorgan were bustled out for 49. It was a farcical game, in which Martin Young was the only player to score a boundary in the entire match.

The other example was at Derby in August 1966, when the contest took place in gale force winds, interspersed with heavy downpours. The storms actually prevented a start from being made until 4.30 p.m. on the first day, and then there were two further stoppages as we made 32 for 2. Conditions were even worse on the second day, and allowed us to play for just seventy minutes, during which we advanced the score to 84 for 3. The sun was shining on the third day, so play started on time, but the wicket was a real sticky dog. We declared at 99 for 6 before Derbyshire responded by declaring on 52 for 1 after batting for forty-five minutes. We started batting again at about 2 p.m., by which time the wicket was starting to cut up and, with a lot of good fortune, we managed to make 73 for 3 in seventy-five minutes, before declaring again and leaving Derbyshire a target of 119 in the remaining ninety minutes. By now the surface was in a dreadful state, and David Allen and Mike Bissex bowled Derbyshire out for 58, with Allen taking 5 for 25 in 7 overs and Bissex 3 for 0 in 3.3 overs. It had been another victory for the 'Glorious Glosters' but, like the win against the South Africans in 1960, it was something of a hollow victory given the conditions.

The cricket calendar in the 1950s and 1960s also saw the counties visit a far wider number of grounds than those frequented by the current professionals. I was lucky to play on a number of beautiful outgrounds, especially those that staged annual festivals and, for me, whether it was as an umpire or a player, I always thought it was better when there was a bit of a buzz around the ground, or a festive feel to a match, with a chance after play to wander into the marquees, meet up with former players and old friends, or simply to mingle with the spectators and players and to talk about the day's events. Scarborough, Tunbridge Wells, Cheltenham, Arundel and Swansea were probably my top five, but I must not forget my home town ground of Dean Park, Bournemouth. It holds a special place in my memory for other reasons, as it was there as a schoolboy that I watched some of the greatest batsmen in county cricket – Len Hutton, Cyril Washbrook, Denis Compton and Bill Edrich. In 1962 Gloucestershire visited Dean Park to play Hampshire, and many of my friends and family turned up to watch. On the last day they saw a thrilling finish, as Gloucestershire chased 244 to win. Arthur Milton batted superbly and, thanks to his efforts, he kept us in the hunt. Arthur was 60 or so not out when I joined him at the crease with 32 runs still needed in seventeen minutes.

Before I went out, I asked Tom Pugh what I should do. 'Block it out for a draw' were his words, but soon after arriving at the crease I realised that, with a bit of luck, we could still get the runs. Arthur was still going well, and I didn't want his efforts to be wasted. I didn't want to disappoint the large crowd either, so I opened my shoulders, hit 2 sixes and 3 fours, and got us home with minutes to spare and still 2 wickets in hand. The crowd had seen a thrilling finish and, although Tom Pugh praised me for my efforts, he also gave me a bit of a ticking off for defying his orders. I felt quite upset about that, especially as we had managed to win, and I have always felt it is important for sportsmen to entertain the crowd, whether it is playing cricket or football.

Another example of putting the crowd first came in what was, without any shadow of doubt, the most memorable match I ever played in – the famous Gillette Cup semi-final of 1971 that saw Lancashire defeat us at Old Trafford at 9 p.m. at night and all in quite the worst light I have ever experienced on a cricket field. The game was televised and, over the years, the BBC have replayed this magnificent game many times, as there was enough action and drama to illustrate the vagaries of this great game. Thirty thousand spectators were present, with hundreds sitting on the grass at the Manchester ground. However, the weather delayed the start, making it inevitable that we would have a late finish and, after winning the toss, Tony Brown opted to bat first. Mike Procter made 65 before being caught by Farokh Engineer off Peter Lever's bowling, and Ron Nicholls made 53 as Gloucestershire amassed 229 for 7 in their 60 overs. Lancashire's target was therefore a shade under 4 an over, but their batsmen were restricted from scoring by some fine bowling by Procter and Brown, while Jack Davey, the jovial Devonian, also bowled a fine spell to contain the Lancashire stroke-makers.

There were still several overs to go as the sun set over the west of the ground and, with the sky becoming darker and darker, the two umpires, Dickie Bird and Arthur Jepson, called over Tony Brown and Jack Bond, the Lancashire captain, who was at the crease at the time. The fielders were having difficulty picking up the ball, while the batsmen had the slight advantage of the sightscreens, but even so, Lancashire still needed 27 runs off the last 4 overs. However, Jack opted to continue as he did not want to disappoint the crowd and have to come back the next day and finish the game in front of an empty stadium. No sooner had the decision to continue been made than David Hughes arrived at the crease and, in the space of a remarkable four minutes, he scored 4, 6, 2, 2, 4 and 6 in an over from John Mortimore, and Lancashire had won – watched by thousands on TV, with the BBC delaying the normal evening news schedule so that the finish could be broadcast live.

We could not believe the sudden turnaround in the game, and we trooped off in a quite shell-shocked state to our dressing room. The kindly meant gesture of the Lancashire players in sending in a tray of glasses filled with champagne only succeeded in rubbing salt into our wounds, and we later headed back home to Bristol, still not quite believing this remarkable turnaround. It had reminded us though of two important things – firstly, that you can never be certain of anything until the game is actually over, and secondly, that you should never forget the crowd, with professional cricket, besides being a wonderful way of life, being a form of entertainment and pleasure for so many people of all ages.

Looking back, I never regretted my decision to concentrate on cricket from the early 1960s, especially as it was through cricket that I met my then wife Gillian. I had been coaching in South Africa in the winter of 1964/65, and was travelling home on the Transvaal Castle when I met her. She was working as a nursery nurse and, on the thirteen-day journey back home, we found plenty of time to see each other.

After making another trip on the boat to and from South Africa, Gillian joined me in Bristol, living with my Gloucestershire colleague David Allen and his wife Joyce. On 17 September 1965 we were married in Derby, Gillian's home town, and after another winter coaching in South Africa, Gillian and I set up home in Mangotsfield. On 16 January 1967 our first child, Stephen Barrie, was born. Two more followed – Christopher John and Adrian Michael – in the space of the next two years and I'm glad to say all three are still thriving.

FIVE

From White Flannels
to White Coat

In 1971 Gloucestershire granted me a Benefit year. It was a sign that my playing days were drawing to a close and, like countless other county professionals before and since, I started to plan my calendar of events. Benefit years are a way for the county clubs to recognise the loyalty and work that you have put in for the club, usually in the ten years or so after you have received your county cap and been a regular member of the county side. The Benefit year also helps to create a nest egg for the future and, in my case, I was very fortunate to gross £8,000. It was quite a tidy sum in those days and was a new Gloucestershire record, surpassing the sum raised for Tom Graveney.

It also reflected the hard work put in by my chairman John Budd, as well as by John Higson, with whom I have remained good friends. My Benefit match took place at Cheltenham against Worcestershire on 7, 9 and 10 August. A decent crowd turned up each day, but sadly the weather intervened and, on the final day, the rain prevented us from bowling out Worcestershire who, at 51 for 3 in their second innings, were chasing 337 to win on a tricky wicket which, like most in my time at the College Ground, helped the spin bowlers. Play eventually got under way at 5 p.m. but, although we pressed hard, we could not take the 7 wickets in the 20 overs of play, as Glenn Turner, the visitors' captain and opening batsman, carefully marshalled his side towards the safety of a draw.

My mind had started to turn towards staying in the game and umpiring. I had enjoyed officiating while coaching at schools in South Africa, so I found out what was needed to become a first-class umpire. At the same time, Gloucestershire asked me to stay on the staff in 1972 and captain the Second XI. I accepted their offer, but I knew that it would just be a temporary post as my heart was now set on umpiring and, after applying officially to the MCC at Lord's, I was delighted when I received a letter from their secretary to say that my application to join the first-class umpires' list had been accepted for 1973. As it turned out, Freddie Jakeman and Johnny Arnold had both decided to retire at the end of the 1972 season and Henry Horton, the former Hampshire and Worcestershire batsman, and myself were appointed as their replacements. Most new umpires started off with a quiet game at Oxford or Cambridge, and I was no different, with the MCC appointing me to stand at Fenner's for Cambridge's games against Yorkshire and Northamptonshire. I was lucky enough to make my umpiring bow with John Langridge – one of the most respected umpires the game has ever had and, at the time, one of the senior umpires on the list and a Test umpire. John was a true gentleman who cut a calm and authoritative figure as an umpire. As a player, I had always found him to be a very genial fellow as well, always willing to have a chat after play and, on several occasions after I had made a good catch or stumping, John would quietly pass on a word of praise out in the middle. This reflected both John's enthusiasm and his appreciation of the game being played in the proper manner. I could have had no finer role model than John as we sat together in the Cambridge pavilion getting ready for play to start.

As it turned out, my first day as a first-class umpire happened to be quite cool and overcast and, after overnight rain, the wicket and the surrounds were quite damp. John and I duly went out and had a look for ten minutes or so before the two captains came out. I naturally deferred to John, but he made it clear right from the outset that we stood as equals, that my opinion was as valuable as his and that we were working together as a team. I then said that I felt the pitch was not fit to start playing on. John immediately concurred and we told the captains that there would be a delay.

The game eventually got under way late, with Yorkshire ending up on 247 for 1 at the close, with Geoff Boycott cashing in with 141 against the student attack. Everything seemed to go okay and, having cut my teeth in the Yorkshire match, I felt quite comfortable for the Northants match. Once again, there wasn't much of a problem as Northamptonshire also dominated the university boys, with a young nineteen-year-old called Wayne Larkins completing his maiden century.

Another common practice the MCC had with new umpires was not to allocate new officials to stand in matches involving their old counties until a couple of years had passed. This was to allow the 'novice' umpire to properly settle in and not be immediately put under pressure by friends and county colleagues. It meant that, for a while, I did not stand in any Gloucestershire games, but when I stood in the match at Southport between Lancashire and Hampshire, I bumped into Barry Richards who by now was playing for Hampshire. It was great to see Barry again, having spent some time with him when he was on Gloucestershire's books in 1965. However, he entered the game in a poor patch of form and, when we met up before the start of play, I mentioned this to him. 'Don't worry, I promise that I'll get you some today,' he replied. Well, he certainly lived up to his promise by producing some majestic batting, adding 280 with Gordon Greenidge in a partnership that was complete carnage, with Barry unleashing some ferocious cover drives, pulls and cuts.

In my first few months, I got a chance to stand with some of the other top umpires on the first-class list – men like Tom Spencer, Charlie Elliott, Arthur Fagg, Jack Crapp and Arthur Jepson, who had all been outstanding county players before rising to the top of the umpiring world. Like me, Jepson also had a football background, having kept goal for Port Vale, Mansfield Town, Stoke City and Lincoln City, as well as playing county cricket with Nottinghamshire. In fact, he's still the only person to have made over 100 League appearances and taken over 1,000 wickets. Arthur and I had often found time when we came across each other on the county circuit to have a yarn after play about various football topics, and I'd always found him to be an affable chap off the pitch. On the field, he was a strong disciplinarian, and gave short shrift to anyone who made a frivolous appeal. Indeed, Arthur did not tolerate any nonsense whatsoever, as shown by his comments in one game where he had become extremely irritated by a particular player who had been fielding at mid-off, from where he had made some less than complimentary remarks when Arthur had turned down several appeals for lbw. When this player came in to bat and asked for his guard, Arthur looked at him and said, 'Shall I give it to you correctly from my position here directly behind the wicket, or from that very funny angle over there where you were standing at mid-off!?'

There were also a host of other real characters on the list at that time, men like dear old Eddie Phillipson, who early each season would gleefully tell anyone who would listen that he would be the first to 100 lbw's for the season, and 'Cec' Pepper, who once turned down a forceful appeal from Ashley Mallett, the fine Australian spinner, and then told the bowler in

forthright term 'You're aiming at just three sticks in the ground, not a flip-
pin' row of railings!' Bill Alley, the former Somerset all-rounder, was another
forthright and no-nonsense umpire who, when answering an lbw appeal
in the affirmative, often sent the batsman on his way with the words, 'Jeez,
what an awful shot – that's out!'

I therefore had a lot of different styles to watch, but I was determined to
be my own man and to do things in my own way. But, to be honest, I don't
think that I was very good at first. Nevertheless, I was appointed to quarter-
final ties in both the Benson & Hedges Cup and Gillette Cup, and somehow
I managed to stay on the panel for 1974. Back in those first few months as
an umpire, I lacked a certain amount of self-belief, but everything changed
after a county match involving Surrey. There was some blatant time-wasting
going on so, after a few overs of this, I decided to take action. I called over
the two captains and told them that what they were doing was a disgrace,
and that if they did not stop wasting time, I would report them to Lord's. It
was the first time that I had spoken so firmly on the field, and I'm sure that
this helped to get me respect.

As the season progressed, I began to feel more comfortable, although now
as an umpire I did not have the administrative support that I had enjoyed
as a player. I had to book my own accommodation for the various fixtures,
and make my own travelling arrangements. I also started to receive feed-
back from the captains' reports, and in particular the marks out of ten that
they were awarding each umpire. At the end of my first season, I averaged
6.29 for the three-day games, and was fifteenth in the table of twenty-six
umpires, while for the one-day games my marks were higher, with an average of 6.47 and a seventh place in the table.

Being a new umpire these days is very different as all potential candidates for the first-class list now have to cut their teeth on the reserve panel
before being promoted, if a vacancy arises, onto the full list. The people
on the reserve list will usually stand in university games, various one-day
games – usually those involving a Minor County side – and perhaps the
odd first-class county match, especially if somebody on the first-class list is
ill or indisposed. Nevertheless, they are still reported upon and their performance marked by the captains, so that the ECB can make an assessment
of their overall performance, and suitability for promotion onto the full list.
As with my first game, it is still the common custom for a new face on the
full list to start their full-time umpiring career standing with a highly experienced umpire. That was the situation back in 1996 when Tony Clarkson,

the former Somerset and Yorkshire all-rounder, came onto the first-class list, and we stood together in the opening round of Benson & Hedges Cup matches in Warwickshire's match with Leicestershire at Edgbaston. It was also Shaun Pollock's first appearance for the county, and both he and Tony had debuts to remember.

Tony was standing at Shaun's end as the Springbok fast bowler roared in, eager to make an impression. With only 2 runs on the board, Vince Wells was caught in the outfield, and then 2 for 1 became 9 for 2 as Gregor Macmillan edged to slip, with Tony correctly checking with me to confirm that the ball had carried into the fielder's hands before raising his finger to send the Leicestershire man back to the pavilion. It immediately became 9 for 3 as with the next delivery James Whitaker was bowled by Pollock. Then, next ball, Phil Robinson spliced a brute of a delivery into short-leg's hands and to the next delivery Darren Maddy miscued straight to Dominic Ostler to give Pollock a remarkable four in four. 'Is it always as dramatic as this?' beamed Tony as we talked in the middle.

Another recent change, and a good one at that, is the introduction of both the first-class and reserve list umpires into Second XI cricket. One of the 'listed' umpires will stand with a local umpire chosen by the home county for Second XI matches. Before 1989, a member of the first-class panel would only stand in these games if he volunteered to do so, and the switch to mandatory appointments came after a thorough investigation into the state of Second XI cricket by Mike Vockins, the Worcestershire secretary. Apparently the local men were unable to instil discipline in the players, and we were told that the appointment of a first-class or reserve list umpire was to give some confidence to the local chap and give them further experience of how the game can be controlled by a top-class umpire.

From my point of view, I found it extremely beneficial because it allowed me to pick up a few tips from them. Many were working men who were true enthusiasts and had many years of league and club experience behind them. It just proved again that the two umpires standing together should always work together, and a reminder that each game involves three teams – the two sides in opposition, with the umpires and scorers forming the third.

In my opinion, two of the very best umpires that I had the pleasure of working with were Dickie Bird and David Shepherd. Both were very pro-fessional and respected worldwide, but they were very different in character. Dickie was very serious-minded, and it was quite hard chatting to him just before the start of a Test. He would fidget, play with his hair and flick himself with talcum powder until the pavilion bell rang and we took the field for the start of the match. Once the game was under way, Dickie's manner changed and, as the session progressed, he became more and more relaxed. In all, I stood in seven Tests with Dickie, as well as a couple of World Cup finals and numerous other one-day internationals and domestic knock-out matches. In all of these Dickie was always the same, and I knew that my role would be to deal with any situation concerning the pitch, the light or the weather.

As for dear old 'Shep' – what a contrast in character to Dickie, but he had just the same qualities and the necessary ingredients to become so popular, well respected and a top umpire. His strengths, I felt, were that he was always ready to communicate on the field, and was always available to help out in awkward moments. I had known 'Shep' for many years as a player with Gloucestershire. When he first arrived on the county's staff in the mid-1960s, he was the young Devon boy who batted in his own way – he was good at it too, scoring a century against Oxford University on his debut in 1965. He remained that way throughout his playing career, before retiring in 1979. In fact, 'Shep' made his umpiring debut with me in a game at The Parks between Oxford University and Glamorgan in 1981. He asked me for all sorts of advice before, during and after the game, but I managed to persuade him that he should make his own decisions and be his own man. He took this to heart, and soon became one of the country's best umpires. My only sadness was that I never got the chance to stand with him in a Test. We shared one knock-out final at Lord's, and three one-day internationals, as well as many other domestic matches, but never a Test.

There was, though, one other very special match when 'Shep' and I were together as the umpires – that was on 24 July 1985 when Gloucestershire played the Australians at Bristol. It was a very special day for the county as we were all introduced to Diana, Princess of Wales, who was Patron of the county. It had been specially organised by the TCCB that two former Gloucestershire players would stand in this match, and it was a very special day that will live in my memory forever.

The men that I stood with during my twenty-five years as an umpire were all excellent colleagues and I have been happy to work with each and every one of them. Obviously, one often has a better rapport with one person than another – that's human nature, and you can sometimes socialise better with one person than somebody else. A cricketer in a team has ten or eleven colleagues to mix with, and by being regularly with them, and sharing the same experiences, close friendships can develop. For an umpire, each match you will usually stand with a different person – sometimes for the only time that season. If you get on very well with them, and have the same outlook on life and the game with them, it makes for pleasant companionship, especially if you stay in the same hotel or guesthouse.

When retiring from umpiring at the end of the 1997 season, I was able to look back on my time on the first-class list and honestly say how much I had enjoyed being an umpire, and in particular standing with the four men appointed just before me – Ray Julian, David Constant, Ken Palmer and Dickie Bird – the latter being one of the great characters of the county circuit in the past twenty-five years.

STANDING WITH DICKIE

H.D. 'Dickie' Bird was probably the most well known of all the umpires that I stood with during my career. I stood with Dickie for the first time in the middle of June 1974 at Swansea in Glamorgan's match against Northamptonshire. We went on to stand together in eight Test matches, two World Cup finals and five domestic cup finals. Dickie and I also stood in numerous semi-final games in the various knock-out competitions, including the Gillette Cup semi-final of 1977 between Middlesex and Somerset at Lord's. The contest was originally scheduled for 17 August but, when we arrived at the ground on the Wednesday morning, heavy rain was falling and by lunchtime, with pools all over the outfield, we abandoned play for the day.

Two reserve days had been set aside for the game to finish, but it continued to pour down on the Thursday and Friday and, on the latter morning, we were called to the office of Donald Carr, the secretary of the MCC, who was dealing with the arrangements for scheduling the match. There was no bowl-out or tossing of a coin in those days, so Mr Carr told us that he had rearranged the match for three days in the following week, with Dickie and I as umpires and, with the final due to take place at the end of the month, we had to do our best to get the game completed the following week. As we left Mr Carr's office Brian Langley, the assistant secretary, said, 'Don't worry about the game next week, because we'll make all of the appropriate arrangements for the match.' They turned out to be prophetic words indeed!

When we returned to Lord's the following week, the weather was no better. It was still bucketing down on the Thursday and panic was starting to set in but, thankfully, Friday dawned clear and bright. The sun was shining, but Lord's was in a total mess. Despite valiant attempts to dry out the sodden turf, conditions were very poor, but Donald Carr told us to ignore the normal playing conditions for a minimum of 20 overs a side, and to finish the game as soon possible.

Brian Close, the Somerset captain, and Mike Smith, who was standing in for Mike Brearley, the Middlesex captain, who was away for a Test match, were also informed about the conditions. Dickie was chatting to Jim Fairbrother, the groundsman, and I had to sort out some form of schedule with the two captains in order to get the game going. The forecast was for more rain later on that day, so the only chance we had was to play as many overs as possible in the morning. I said to the two captains that we had almost three hours until lunchtime, so we were to get the game started as soon as possible. Somerset wanted 20 overs to bowl and Middlesex wanted just 10, so I decided to split that down the middle and have 15 overs each, with a start at 11 a.m. and a finish at around 1 p.m.

I looked around for Dickie because, as umpires, we were supposed to be conferring together with the captains, and it had to be a joint decision. Dickie eventually arrived and we had to convince him that this was the only possible solution in order to get a positive outcome in the time available. Eventually the game got going, with Somerset going in to bat in a frantic way and being dismissed inside 15 overs for just 59. Middlesex duly went in and got 61 with 4 overs to spare, with the teams trooping off just before 1 p.m. for lunch, having completed the match and got the result that the MCC wanted. While we were having our lunch, there was an enormous crash of thunder and Dickie and I walked out onto the balcony to see the rain pouring down yet again. Within minutes Lord's was completely awash, with seats floating about around the Tavern area. Dickie then turned to me and said, 'Well mate, we got that right, didn't we!?'

In 1986 Dickie and I were standing in a Test at Edgbaston between England and India that was interrupted by a political demonstration. Everything was ticking over as normal when a chap ran onto the field waving a huge banner, on which were printed the words 'Metso must stay' – a reference to Mr Metso Montcrieffe, a twenty-five-year-old Jamaican who was facing deportation, with the protest being engineered to show disagreement with the British Government's decision. Dickie and I decided not to tackle the chap, so we stood back and waited for a steward, a policeman or an official to walk onto the field and sort matters out. But then, as we were waiting in the middle of the pitch, a young woman called Joanna Daniels walked up to the wicket at my end, took off the two bails and dropped them down inside her tracksuit trousers. I went up to reason with her as I couldn't see why the heck she should have my bails, then I heard the protestor, Mr Pervaiz Khan, warn me not to touch the young woman. Phil Edmonds then chipped in, 'Go on B.J. You're in charge of the game. Go on, get your bails back!' There was a fair bit of mirth on the square as I escorted the young lady halfway to the pavilion, when a young policewoman called Lorraine Arscott saved the day. I had often seen Lorraine at games when she was off-duty and I recognised her as a keen Warwickshire supporter. Lorraine persuaded the protestor to return the bails to me and, with the protest completed, we duly got on with the game. The two intruders were detained by the police over-night, and I heard that Joanna Daniels was in floods of tears as soon as she got off the field having made her protest about Mr Montcrieffe.

In 1979 I was appointed to stand in the Prudential World Cup. The 1979 competition was the second World Cup and, before everything began, all of the players, officials and twelve umpires met up at Lord's for an introduction parade before we were bussed off to Buckingham Palace where we had the honour of meeting Her Majesty the Queen.

Fortunately, the competition was blessed with reasonably good weather, and I began by standing with David Constant in England's match against Australia at Lord's on 9 June. Then it was England against Canada at Old Trafford with John Langridge on 13 June, followed by New Zealand against the West Indies at Trent Bridge with Dickie Bird. Apart from the match with Canada, all of the games were fine contests, each with their moments of tension and turnarounds. Just when it seemed one set of bowlers were poised to win the game for their team, two batsmen would make a stand and pull their side out of the mire. It had been fascinating to watch the different teams, some I had not seen before, battling it out with skill, good captaincy, craftsmanship and gamesmanship.

After the group stages ended, a knockout stage began on 16 June and, as a relatively new face at international level, I was satisfied to have stood in the group matches. To my complete astonishment and utter delight, I was then told that I had been selected to stand in the final at Lord's on 23 June alongside Dickie Bird. It was a great honour to be chosen for the match and, soon after breakfast on 23 June, I joined Dickie in the umpires' room at Lord's. Dickie was always quite nervous prior to a game, and he was soon pacing around the small room, throwing talcum powder over his body to cool off. For a while, we spoke about how we would approach the game, and deal with any potential situations that may arise. This helped to calm us both down but, even so, it was still a nerve-racking moment, walking out onto the hallowed turf in front of tens of thousands of spectators, and many millions watching on television. My stomach felt as though a couple of million butterflies were having a party there as we walked out from the pavilion, but I had to appear to be cool, calm and collected, and completely in charge of the situation. Jim Fairbrother, the highly experienced Lord's groundsman, was standing out in the middle at the Pavilion End to greet us and hand over the pitch to us. As we approached him, Dickie said, 'Well, Jimmy lad – this is a big occasion for us and they chose us because we are the best. We're here to umpire a top game of cricket, and we're here because we're the best, and don't forget that lad!' Dickie then shook hands with me and walked off towards the Nursery End. In those days, the main camera was situated at the Pavilion End, and I quickly realised that I would have the TV cameras over my shoulder for the rest of the game. I therefore learned two valuable lessons from Dickie that day – the art of puffery and the most comfortable end to umpire from!

The game proved to be utterly absorbing. The West Indies batted first and England started quite well, as the Caribbean side slipped to 99 for 4. Then came a remarkable partnership between Viv Richards and Collis King, with the latter playing some amazing shots, scoring 86 out of the 139 runs added in a shade over seventy-five minutes. England had opted to go in with just four front-line bowlers – Ian Botham, Mike Hendrick, Chris Old and Phil Edmonds, and their three 'make-up' bowlers – Graham Gooch, Wayne Larkins and Geoff Boycott – bore the brunt of King's fusillade.

Chasing 286 for 9, England began quite well with Mike Brearley and Geoff Boycott putting on 129, but they used up too many overs in achieving this position, and placed a bit of a strain on the remaining batsmen who had to go for quick runs right from the off. It proved to be too much against some fine West Indian bowling, as Michael Holding finished with 2 for 16 and big Joel Garner 5 for 38. However, it was Viv Richards who won the Man of the Match award for his 138.

It had been a very exciting and exhausting day, and there was much celebrating after the West Indies had retained the World Cup. I was pleasantly tired as the whole match had required total concentration and my reaction,

1983 World Cup umpires. From left to right, back row: David Constant, Barrie Meyer, Barrie Leadbeater, Merv Kitchen, Roy Palmer, David Shepherd, Don Oslear, Alan Whitehead. Front row: Ken Palmer, Dickie Bird, David Evans and Jack Birkenshaw.

on returning to the dressing room at the end of the game, was one of relief that there were no untoward or controversial moments. We must have done a pretty good job as, four years later, Dickie and I were chosen again to umpire the 1983 World Cup final.

Once again, twelve English umpires were chosen to stand in the zonal matches. My first appointment was standing with Don Oslear for the game at The Oval between England and New Zealand on 9 June. It turned out to be a comfortable victory for England as Allan Lamb made 103 out of England's 322 for 6, before Bob Willis took 2 for 9 in 7 overs. Then it was off to Lord's on 13 June to officiate with Alan Whitehead in England's contest against Pakistan, which saw Zaheer Abbas make a fine 83 not out as his side made 193 for 8 in their 60 overs. But it proved not to be enough as England completed another easy win, cruising home with 8 wickets in hand and 9.2 overs to spare, with Graeme Fowler batting throughout to make 78. Two days later I stood with David Shepherd at The Oval in the match between the West Indies and India. Run-scoring was not that easy and, for once, even the flamboyant Viv Richards was subdued, but he did enough to help lay the foundation of a total of 282 for 9. It proved to be a winning total as India were then bowled out for 216 to give the West Indies victory by 66 runs.

I had another chance to see the Indians in action as my next game was their match against Zimbabwe at Tunbridge Wells, and what a match it turned out to be, highlighting the vagaries of the game. Zimbabwe made an early breakthrough as Sunil Gavaskar fell leg before for a duck with his side on 6 for 2. It soon became 6 for 3, then 9 for 4 and 17 for 5 as the Zimbabwean bowlers scythed through the opposition top order. After a quick rally more wickets fell as India slipped further to 78 for 7 and the Zimbabweans, the minnows of the competition, were sensing a dramatic and largely unexpected victory. It seemed as if there would be no way back for the Indians, but their captain Kapil Dev stayed put and, with Roger Binny, he embarked on what can only be described as General Custer's last stand. With some ferocious blows, Kapil Dev took the score to 140 before Binny was out, but he then received useful support from Syed Kirmani, the wicketkeeper. Kapil continued to smack the ball all around the park and, with Kirmani running some sensible singles, they took the score to 266 for 8 with Kapil finishing on an astonishing 175 not out. He had achieved almost a miracle, pulling his team out of the fire that day and, with Zimbabwe being dismissed for 235, it was largely down to their inspirational captain that India secured a place initially in the semi-final of the Prudential Cup and then, after beating England, a place in the final against the West Indies.

Once again, Dickie and I had been chosen to stand in the final and, together with the two finalists, we stayed the night before the game in the Regent's Park Hotel opposite Lord's. From soon after dawn, the sun was streaming into my bedroom, and Dickie and I were at the ground soon after 8 a.m. to get ready for the great day. As I walked across the road and over to the ground, there were already long queues of people eager to get inside, and it didn't take long for the ground to start buzzing. As in 1979, Dickie and I were both suffering from pre-match tension, so we went through our little pep talk again, before walking out to inspect the wicket. It was hard, true and very flat and, with the ground starting to fill up, Dickie and I walked back to the umpires' room knowing that we were in for a good game.

As I started to get changed, the butterflies started, and I don't believe that a Test Match umpire ever becomes hardened to these pre-match nerves, especially at a ground that is so steeped in history as Lord's. There was a heck of a din as we walked out to the middle, with the West Indians running out behind us to take the field, but my nerves soon subsided as we got the match under way and got totally absorbed in the contest. India could only muster 183 in their innings and, as we walked out again for the West Indian innings, it seemed only a matter of time before they would win the World Cup for the third time. But they seemed rather over-eager and very aggressive, with impossible shots being played against the Indians' very disciplined bowling. In contrast, there was a definite lack of discipline as Greenidge went for 1, Haynes for 13, Clive Lloyd for 8 and Larry Gomes for 5. Viv Richards was still there though and, for a while, there were a few thoughts in my mind that I might witness another astonishing counterattack, just when everything seemed over for the batting side. But it was not to be as Viv got a top edge off Mohinder Amarnath and Kapil Dev took a good catch at mid-wicket. The West Indies were eventually all out for 140, as India won by 43 runs, and I'm still convinced that, had India got a larger total, say 220-230, the result might have been very different as the West Indians would have approached their innings with more caution and more discipline. But, on the day, the Indians were the better team and, by the time we had changed and headed back to our hotel, a great celebration had got under way. Everywhere was choc-a-bloc with happy Indian fans and other well-wishers, while some of the Indian team were joyously wandering around still wearing their whites. As far as Dickie and I were concerned, we were relieved that the game had been played without incident and, after sharing a few drinks with the delirious supporters, we headed up to our rooms knowing that once again it had been a job well done.

What they said about B.J.

Dickie Bird – county and Test umpire
(from *That's Out* – published in 1985 by Arthur Barker Ltd.)

Barrie Meyer and I were the first umpires to use light meters. They were introduced in 1978 largely as a result of an unfortunate incident at Trent Bridge in the Second Test of that year, with New Zealand beaten by an innings. The umpires at Nottingham were David Constant and Tom Spencer. They had a dilemma on the Saturday morning with a light drizzle falling from grey skies. They knew they might have to come off because of the light, but they were also aware that the public were demanding action. In trying to do their best for all concerned they were in an impossible position.

They elected to play, but after only 2 balls had been delivered they realised that the conditions were not after all satisfactory so they brought the players off. Under the regulations, the pitch could not be covered until play had been abandoned for the day and the consequence was that New Zealand eventually had to bat on a wet surface some four hours later. They were dismissed for 120 and understandably felt hard done by as they followed on.

While the pros and cons were being debated, a photographer casually observed that according to his light meter the conditions when play was proceeding in the afternoon had been exactly the same as when they started in the morning. For once, this scientific fact had a real value. It planted the seeds of an important idea in some official minds, and Barrie and I were given a brief lecture on how the meters worked by Patrick Eager, the well-known photographer who specialises so brilliantly in cricket, and we were told to use them in the Third Test at Lord's. No one I imagine will be in the least surprised to learn that the light remained perfect throughout, and we never had to rely on our pocket-sized assistants!

ONE-DAY FINALS

Dickie was my partner when I stood in my first knockout final at Lord's in 1978. It was only my sixth season on the umpires' list, and it was a great privilege to be appointed to stand in the Gillette Cup final, as it was the showpiece match of the year – an indication, if I needed one, that I had come of age as an umpire.

When I first joined the first-class list in 1973, I probably had more experience of playing in one-day games than any of the other officials. The fast and furious pace of these limited-overs contests stood me in good stead and, in my first season on the list, I stood in quarter-final ties of the 55-overs Benson & Hedges Cup competition and the 60-overs Gillette Cup. Both involved Kent who, at the time, had a fine one-day team. In the first contest, under a scorching sun and in front of a capacity crowd at the Northlands Road ground at Southampton, Kent were the victors by 11 runs after a good half-century from Asif Iqbal, their gifted Pakistani all-rounder, supported by some typically accurate bowling from Bob Woolmer and Derek Underwood. They were given a fright, though, by Hampshire's Richard Gilliat who, despite a leg strain, played a true captain's innings with a combative half-century. Coming in lower in the order than usual, he soon put bat to ball, reasoning that his best chance of seeing Hampshire home was to strike boundaries rather than attempt a few singles. The ball was soon disappearing to all parts but, after reaching his fifty with a six, he was well caught by Alan Ealham on the square-leg boundary.

Six weeks later, and in front of a capacity crowd once again, I officiated Kent in their next quarter-final, against Sussex in the Gillette Cup. But this time, the Kent batting never fired as they attempted to chase a target of 264 in their 60 overs – something no team had ever done at that time in the one-day competition. In the face of this record run-chase, Kent slipped to 32 for 4 in the opening dozen overs or so after the home bowlers had made early inroads, notably John Snow who returned the outstanding figures of 7-5-8-2. Ably supported by the Buss brothers – Tony and Mike – Kent were bustled out for 135.

I was not too upset when this contest ended well before the scheduled finish time, as these one-day contests could be long and quite tiring days. My experience in playing in them, plus the long hours I had spent keeping wicket, helped me enormously and concentration over a long period was never a problem. I was pleased to be appointed to officiate in quarter and semi-final ties in these competitions again in the course of the next four years, before getting my first cup final in September 1978 as Sussex played Somerset for the Gillette Cup. The match proved to be a triumph for another loyal member of the wicketkeepers' union – Arnold Long, who had kept with distinction for many years with Surrey and now Sussex. 'Ob' also took something of a gamble by boldly inviting the strong Somerset batting side to take first use of the wicket. He gambled on his bowlers extracting some help from the overcast and damp conditions, and he was rewarded with Somerset on 129 for 4 at lunch, with the dangerous Viv Richards having fallen just before the interval to a well-judged catch on the deep square-leg boundary by Geoff Arnold, a fellow Surrey old boy.

After the break, Ian Botham boldly took the attack to the Sussex bowlers but, well as Ian hit, 'Ob' carefully restricted his scoring opportunities, and Sussex were left with a target of 208. Somerset's bowlers could not make any impression with the new ball, and a careful innings of 62 not out by Paul Parker saw Sussex home with 41 balls to spare. As far as I was concerned, everything during the game had gone like clockwork and it was a great feeling for me at the end of day to leave the packed headquarters of world cricket knowing that I had done a good job.

Dickie and I stood again at Lord's the following year in the Benson & Hedges Cup final on 21 July. It was a very different match to the previous September, with the high-scoring contest being played on a fast, true wicket in glorious sunshine. The highlight of the game was a superb 120 from Graham Gooch who punished a Surrey attack that was missing its spearhead Sylvester Clarke, and also had another stalwart, Robin Jackman, not fully fit.

My next cup final at Lord's – the 1980 Benson & Hedges Cup final between Essex and Northamptonshire – was altogether a different affair to the first two. For a start, my partner was the admirable David Constant, but the first day of the match, Saturday 19 July, was completely washed out, and it was decided that the game would have to be decided on the Monday. This did not trouble Essex too much as they did not have a Sunday League contest, but Northants had a League match at Wantage Road against Derbyshire, while I had a fixture at Trent Bridge standing with Ron Aspinall in the match between Nottinghamshire and Worcestershire. So, after calling play off at Lord's, I had to travel up the M1 to Nottingham. As it turned out, the Sunday was a quite a wet day as well, with Northamptonshire's match being washed out, but the weather brightened up enough in Nottingham for a 10-over-a-side thrash. Worcestershire duly won by 18 runs and, twenty-four hours or so after heading north up the M1, I headed back down to London for the Benson & Hedges final – it proved to be quite a contest. Despite a slightly damp outfield, Northants batted first and, thanks to some accurate Essex bowling and clever field placing by their shrewd captain Keith Fletcher, Northants were dismissed for 209 with their final wicket falling off the penultimate ball. Graham Gooch began well and, by the time the Essex hundred came up, only 1 wicket had fallen. It looked as if it was going to be a repeat of the previous year's final, but then Gooch was caught at the second attempt by Allan Lamb at mid-on. None of the other Essex batsmen were able to maintain the run-scoring tempo that Graham had created and, after the clatter of further wickets, Northants decisively came back into the match, and the nerves started to jangle as we entered the final overs.

At 198 for 7 Essex needed 12 to win off the final over from Sarfraz Nawaz, Northamptonshire's vastly experienced bowler. With the hard-hitting Norbert Philip at the non-strikers' end, it was still possible that Essex could reach their target, but Neil Smith, the Essex wicketkeeper, opted to go for the big shots himself rather than push a single and give Philip the strike, and Smith was bowled by the second ball of the over. Ray East, the new batsman, then wisely pushed a single off the next delivery, and Philip blasted two more off the fourth. David Constant and I then conferred before the final two deliveries, because the regulations for this competition meant that if Essex hit 8 more runs, they would have won by losing fewer wickets. We duly informed the two batsmen and Jim Watts, the fielding captain, but Philip then missed the next delivery, and could only get two off the last. As hundreds of jubilant Northants supporters swarmed onto the outfield, I hastily made my way off the pitch, rather tired after all the events of the previous forty-eight hours, but once again very pleased that this high-profile match had passed by without any difficulties.

Next year, 25 July 1981 saw Dickie Bird back alongside me in the white coat for the Benson & Hedges Cup final between Surrey and Somerset. It was a less tense contest than the one the previous year, but it saw two virtuoso performances by great West Indian cricketers. Firstly Joel Garner, the tall and languid Somerset bowler, took 5 for 14 and crippled the talented Surrey batting with a bowling performance as fine as any I have seen over the years in a knockout final. He began by taking a single wicket in an economical opening spell, as Surrey limped to 16 for 1 in the first 16 overs, with their top order rendered almost impotent by Joel's high bounce and devilish swing. Later in the innings, he returned to pick up 4 more wickets at almost no cost, with a couple of victims falling to his trademark yorker. Joel's figures at the time were the best in the B&H final and, as Dickie and I took the field for the Somerset innings, it looked likely that that Joel would secure the Gold Award. But his Caribbean compatriot Viv Richards then produced another innings of rare brilliance, hitting an unbeaten 132 with the full range of audacious and powerful shots as Somerset cruised to their target of 195. Viv's reward for his breathtaking innings was the Man of the Match award, leaving Joel empty-handed after his outstanding spell.

The following year I saw further excellent bowling spells in knockout matches, starting with Robin Jackman's 6 for 22 in the NatWest Trophy quarter-final at Southampton. The veteran Surrey seamer fully exploited the overcast and damp conditions and, with a 10 a.m. start, Hampshire's fate was probably sealed when they lost the toss and were put in. It was a similar story at Lord's on the first Saturday in September, although this time the Warwickshire top order offered more resistance to the lively Surrey new-ball attack of Jackman and Sylvester Clarke, the West Indian paceman. But the match-winner for Surrey in the 1982 final was David Thomas, the brisk left-arm seamer, who filleted the Warwickshire middle order to finish with figures of 3 for 26 from his 11 overs and, after Alan Butcher had guided Surrey to their target, Thomas deservedly picked up the Man of the Match award.

While the 1982 NatWest final was a very one-sided affair, the B&H final the following year, in which Dickie and I were again in charge, was a very different and tense affair. Early morning drizzle had delayed the start of the match by fifty minutes and, after losing the toss, Middlesex's batsmen were soon struggling as the Essex attack gained assistance off the pitch and in the air. But Clive Radley, the vastly experienced Middlesex batsman, then dropped anchor, and his unbeaten 89 guided Middlesex to a decent total of 196. But when tea was taken at 6.20 p.m., Essex were 113 for 1 and it looked as if they would comfortably reach the target.

While in the pavilion, Dickie and I checked the match regulations that allowed for a match when the start had been delayed to reach a conclusion that night after the scheduled close of play, as long as the light remained good and, in our opinion, did not disadvantage either side. Before going out we reminded the two captains of this playing condition, and said that, if things deteriorated, we would have to return on the reserve day. Thankfully, the light held and, at 8.15 p.m., with only a handful of overs left, I felt that the right thing would be for the match to continue. Dickie agreed, and the final few overs were played out in rising tension. By this time, the jitters had started to affect the Essex batting. They had experienced some bad luck in losing Keith Pont as he dropped his bat onto the stumps after being hit on the helmet by a rising short ball from Neil Williams. At 185 for 5 with 24 balls still remaining, it looked as if Essex would still score the 12 runs they needed. But Mike Gatting's astute captaincy then came into its own as he stifled Essex's lower order. Norman Cowans, the England paceman, also produced a fine late burst, supported by some excellent out-fielding by his Middlesex colleagues. John Carr, the twelfth man, came on and took an excellent running catch at deep mid-on, while Mike Gatting at short mid-wicket parried a fierce pull by David East against a short ball from Cowans and, to the delight of his teammates, 'Gatt' clung onto the rebound. Then Clive Radley at short cover ran out Ray East as he attempted a single, and Cowans clean bowled Neil Foster as Middlesex completed a dramatic victory by 4 runs.

Two years later, David Constant and I were in charge of another nail-biter and an even closer finish in the final of the 1985 NatWest Trophy. Essex were involved once again, but this time they batted first and their talented top order responded with 280 for 2 in 60 overs. Remarkably for a one-day game, there was not a single wide or no-ball in the Essex innings as Brian Hardie, the Scotsman, clubbed a forthright 110 before being run out, while Graham Gooch produced another high-quality innings of 91 before being bowled by Andy Pick. Tim Robinson and Chris Broad then added 143 for the first wicket but, after Broad had been run out, the Nottinghamshire innings faltered and more wickets fell as the Notts batsmen tried to force the pace. With 37 needed off the last 3 overs, Essex looked home and hosed, but Derek Randall, the mercurial Notts and England batsman, improvised brilliantly and garnered enough of the strike to bring the equation down to 18 off the final over from Derek Pringle. Randall continued to play cheekily, moving extravagantly across to the off-side to counter Pringle's leg-stump line, and he was rewarded with 16 astonishing runs from the first 5 deliveries. With the tension reaching fever pitch, Pringle then bowled a low full toss but, as Randall moved inside the line to this final delivery, he became rather tucked up, and Paul Prichard was perfectly placed at mid-wicket to hold onto Randall's stroke to give Essex a thrilling 1-run victory.

All of these finals had been quite pleasant affairs and, although being very tense at times, they had all passed by without any controversy. How different it was in my next and last one-day final on 10 July 1993 as I stood with David Shepherd in the Benson & Hedges Cup final between Lancashire and Derbyshire at Lord's. In front of a crowd in excess of 24,000, Derbyshire batted first and started poorly, losing Peter Bowler early on to Philip DeFreitas, but gradually they came back into the match with Chris Adams, Tim O'Gorman and Dominic Cork all stepping up the tempo. A few verbals started to fly around and then, when Chris Adams was facing Wasim Akram, the Derbyshire man was hit on the shoulder by a high full toss from the Pakistani. I immediately called no ball as anything above waist high and a full toss was, like overstepping the crease, not considered as a legal delivery, and in accordance with the playing conditions, I also issued a warning to

Wasim for bowling this ball. Had I believed that he had deliberately bowled a beamer, I was allowed to have stopped him from bowling, but I wasn't sure. Neither was David Shepherd as we conferred while Adams was receiving treatment, so, believing it to have been accidental, we allowed the Pakistani to continue bowling.

Having ascertained from the Derbyshire physiotherapist that Adams was fit enough to continue, I went back to my position behind the stumps and the match duly continued. The chatter between the players and the verbal sledging continued though, and on several occasions, after harsh words had been exchanged between the players, 'Shep' and I had to speak to the players to make it clear that we were not going to put up with this sort of behaviour. It was definitely the most fiercely contested final that I had ever been involved with and, after the match, I became aware that Wasim Akram and Chris Adams had been involved in an altercation in a recent County Championship match at Derby. The game, on 24 June, had been umpired by John Holder and George Sharp, and apparently there had been a dispute about the state of the ball when Lancashire were bowling. John and George had inspected the ball, and had decided that there was nothing wrong with it, but apparently Derbyshire were not happy with this decision, and had taken the matter up with the TCCB who, in turn, had decided that it was unnecessary to take further action.

This incident between Adams and Wasim must have raised the temperature for the Benson & Hedges final and, had I been aware of this previous altercation, I suppose I might have taken a different view of the full toss bowled at Adams. As I was changing after the game, I mulled over the incident again in my mind, wondering whether I had in fact made the right decision to let Wasim continue to bowl. But I didn't have any real evidence that the full toss was deliberate and, in this situation, I would have had to be a very brave man indeed to have taken him off. I reasoned that, as unfortunate an incident as it was, everything had been dealt with out in the middle, and the game was over, with Derbyshire winning by 6 runs.

SIX

International Umpire

During the period between 1978 and 1993, when I officiated in international matches, I rubbed shoulders with the very best, and was fortunate to see some outstanding cricketers play in some outstanding matches. Test matches are the pinnacle of the first-class game, and are far more demanding than standing in domestic county matches. For a start, there is always an element of tension and, naturally, the standard of play is much higher. But as I was standing in England matches, I was still dealing with players with whom I had a good relationship – not only professionally on the field, but also in a more relaxed manner off the field after play.

The nucleus of the England team during that period contained the likes of Ian Botham, David Gower, Graham Gooch, Bob Taylor, Bob Willis, Phil Edmonds, Geoff Boycott, Geoff Miller, John Emburey, John Lever and Mike Gatting. Naturally, they all had different temperaments – some had a ready and quick sense of humour, while others were more serious or reserved. As an umpire at county level, I had got to know how their minds were working, and I soon came to terms with their ways. Some would want you to talk to them, others would prefer for you to wait until they talked to you. I was fortunate, too, that I had spent a lot of time with John Lever who had been regularly travelling out each winter to play and coach in the local leagues in Natal. We often stayed in the same hotel for the season and, in the five or six months that we were out there together, I got to know J.K. very well and built up a good relationship with him.

In 1977 I made my debut in international cricket, standing in the Prudential Trophy one-day international between England and Australia at Old Trafford on 2 June. As well as being a new experience for me, the day was a very enjoyable one and went by with little difficulty as far as I was concerned. All the decisions I had to adjudicate upon were very straightforward, including the one involving Graham Barlow, the Middlesex batsman, who was making his first appearance for England. Barlow was going along very nicely and had reached 42 when his partner, Tony Greig, pushed a ball towards gully and called for a run. Barlow, however, decided that he couldn't make it from his end, so he sent Greig back. But that was not the end of it, because Rodney Marsh, the Australian wicketkeeper, had chased after the ball and, on looking up, saw that Barlow had turned his back on the ball. I saw this happening as I was quite square with the wicket, about ten to twelve feet away from the popping crease, and could see the danger Barlow was in, because he had assumed, strolling back to the non-striker's end, that the ball was going to become dead. Quick as a flash, Marsh pulled off his glove and, from a difficult angle, broke the wicket at my end with a fine throw. Barlow was out of his crease and, after the appeal went up, I raised my finger to give Barlow run out. He departed rather crestfallen, but England went on to win the game by 2 wickets. With so much money sloshing around in football and other professional sports these days, it is interesting to reflect that prize money back in 1977 for the Prudential Trophy was £2,000 for each win, and £250 for the Man of the Series.

I had really enjoyed my first taste of international cricket in 1977. So the following year I was delighted to hear that I had been appointed to stand in the Test match at Edgbaston between England and Pakistan, starting on 1 June. However, during the spring I had been suffering from a stomach complaint, and was on medication by the time the English season started in late April. The problems continued and, on 24 May, during the match between Gloucestershire and Worcestershire at Bristol, I collapsed and was taken to hospital, where it was discovered that I had a perforated ulcer.

As a result, rather than making my Test match debut, I spent the first week of June propped up in bed in the Bristol Royal Infirmary, recovering from an operation and watching the game on television together with some other patients. However, they were oblivious as to who I was, and there was a scene straight out of a *Monty Python* sketch before play on the first morning as Richie Benaud began the commentary. He started in his usual way and then, as the cameras panned over to Kenny Palmer, who had taken my place, Richie mentioned that I was in hospital recovering from an operation, and he wished me a speedy recovery. I immediately said, 'Thanks

Richie' and all of my fellow patients looked around in astonishment! It took a few minutes for me to explain that I was the bloke to whom Richie was referring, but we soon settled down to watch the play, with me frequently being called upon to give my expert opinion to the rest of the ward!

Fortunately I soon recovered and, thanks to Kenny Palmer's kindness in swapping Tests, I was able to stand later in the summer in two of England's Tests against New Zealand – the First Test at The Oval with David Constant and the Third Test at Lord's with Dickie Bird.

The morning of 27 July 1978 saw me make my way across London to the Kennington Oval to make my debut as a Test umpire. I arrived at the historic ground two hours or so before the start and, after saying good morning to the stewards, and to some of the England and New Zealand players who had arrived to practise, I made my way to the umpire's room. As I was feeling a little bit apprehensive, I was eager to have a chat with my colleague David Constant, who had established himself as one of our country's top umpires. I was, as a newcomer to Test cricket, hoping for a few tips from 'Connie' but, as I got changed, there was no sign of him and, as time went by, I got progressively more anxious as I sat in the umpire's room waiting for 'Connie' to arrive.

There was an hour or so before the match was due to start when 'Connie' arrived – as ever, cheerful and ready to get into action. I quickly told him that I would welcome some advice as it was my first Test, to which he replied with a big smile on his face, 'Barrie, you have been appointed to umpire a Test match – it's as simple as that,' correctly reminding me that being appointed in the first place was a huge vote of confidence.

As far as our decision-making was concerned, it proved to be a very straightforward game. England eventually won by 7 wickets, recovering from the loss, to the third ball of their first innings, of Graham Gooch, who I gave out after Brendon Bracewell, the eighteen-year-old Kiwi fast bowler, had trapped the Essex batsman leg-before. There was always something in the wicket for the bowlers, but David Gower made a fine century to give England a 45-run lead. By the time the tourists had wiped off the arrears, they had already lost three top-order batsmen as Bob Willis and Ian Botham perfectly exploited the humid conditions. The fourth day was completely washed out as around an inch and a half of rain fell during a prolonged storm over the ground. With the weather forecasters having predicted torrential downpours, the Surrey authorities had borrowed some additional tarpaulins from the All England tennis club at Wimbledon, so when 'Connie' and I inspected the pitch first thing on the final day, we were pleased to decide that play could start on time. The Kiwis stubbornly launched a rearguard action, but England's spinners, Geoff Miller and Phil Edmonds, cleverly handled by the shrewd Mike Brearley, steadily worked their way through the rest of the batting, leaving England with a target of 138. Richard Hadlee and young Bracewell produced a hostile new-ball spell before a flamboyant 91 from Graham Gooch saw England home.

Richard Hadlee and Ian Botham produced some outstanding bowling in my next Test appearance in the third and final match of the series, at Lord's during the last week of August. Richard took 7 wickets, while Ian had a match haul of 11, and recorded second-innings figures of 5 for 39 as the tourists were bustled out for just 67. Ian swung the ball in such an alarming way that he was virtually unplayable and, after his devastating spell, England romped to a 7-wicket win.

The game wasn't completely devoid of incident as far as Dickie and I were concerned as, in the New Zealand first innings, Dickie had to warn Ian Botham for bowling a nasty bumper to Stephen Boock, the Kiwi tail-ender and a non-recognised batsman. Ian had bowled a long spell, during which he had finally removed Geoff Howarth, who had overcome illness to score a fine 123. Whether it was Ian relieving his frustration or just a show of exuberance, his bouncer at Boock was uncalled for and, after a nod in my direction at square leg, Dickie quickly stepped in and called over Mike Brearley. The England captain told Dickie that there would be no repetition and, after a word with Mike, Ian resumed bowling, and the game continued without any more incident.

My next Test match involving New Zealand saw me inadvertently share with them in a moment of cricket history for the Kiwis. The game in question was the Second Test of their 1983 series in England, and the match at Headingley saw the tourists record their first ever Test victory on English soil. It was only after the match had finished that I became aware that they had ended a long run of 17 defeats and 11 draws, thanks to innings of 93 and 84 respectively from openers John Wright and Bruce Edgar, plus a forthright 75 from Richard Hadlee who, remarkably, went wicket-less in this historic match for his country. However, his efforts with the bat saw New Zealand secure an invaluable first-innings lead of 152, and then Lance Cairns, with his first-ever 10-wicket match haul, plus a 5-wicket burst from Ewan Chatfield in England's second innings, helped the Kiwis to win by 5 wickets shortly after tea on the fourth day.

At the time, the umpires had to share the showers in the visitors' dressing room so, after David Constant and I had got undressed, we had to make our way through the New Zealanders' dressing room in order to grab a shower. To say that the tourists were thrilled at having won would be the biggest understatement of the year, as they were singing away merrily and toasting a famous victory in the annals of New Zealand's sporting history. Both David and I knew several of the touring team quite well, as they were regulars on the county circuit. After stopping for a brief word of congratulation, Jeremy Coney, the delightful New Zealand captain, and the rest of the team insisted that we stayed in their dressing room and join in with their party – a very unusual but thoroughly enjoyable way to finish the Test!

In 1987 I was involved, together with colleague Alan Whitehead, in a rather embarrassing situation during the second day of the Fourth Test against Pakistan at Edgbaston. It was a particularly overcast day and play had been delayed by bad light and drizzle until 1.25 p.m. There had already been further stoppages by mid-afternoon and it was after one of these that Alan and I had come out from the umpires' room on the side of the pavilion, only to walk out to the middle and to be left standing on our own, waiting for the England fielders to appear. After three or four minutes there was still no sign of them but, by now, the light had deteriorated again and, after looking at our light meters, Alan and I returned to the pavilion with the England team still nowhere in sight. It later transpired that nobody in the England team had been keeping a lookout from their changing room – presumably it ought to have been the twelfth man – and, on a day when there was limited action, the Press made much of England's non-appearance. The blame was apportioned in several directions, with some people suggesting that Alan and I had been at fault for not informing the England dressing room of our decision.

As Christopher Martin-Jenkins wrote in *The Cricketer* magazine, 'It is not true that no rule or law obliges the umpires to tell the players to go out, because law three, section eight states that immediately the umpires decide that play is possible they shall call upon the players to resume the game. Clearly therefore they should have done so, but this oversight neither explains nor condones the failure of the England team to keep an eye on what was going on in the middle, especially as the light was clearly getting better even as they went off the field. It demonstrated an insensitivity to the crowd too. The players must never forget that countless thousands of ordinary people care passionately about the success or failure of the England

cricket team. They should never be seen to care anything less than passionately themselves.'

Such an embarrassing event would never happen in Tests these days, as
there are now so many liaison staff, plus a third and fourth umpire, to help
relay information to the players and others who need to know. Another
change has been the introduction of a match referee, appointed by the ICC.
In fact, I stood with Merv Kitchen in the first Test match in England in
which a referee was appointed – the game in question was the First Test
of the 1992 series with Pakistan, at the Edgbaston ground in Birmingham.
Bob Cowper, the former Australian Test player, had been appointed as the
referee, but he had little to do as the match passed by without too much
incident concerning the players.

However, it wasn't devoid of incident as far as Merv and I were concerned.
Once again, the West Midlands weather interrupted the proceedings, with
rain washing out the first day's play. It was still quite damp and overcast the
following morning, ruling out any prospect of play before lunch. Midway
through the afternoon, Merv and I got the game under way, but it was still
very overcast and, after just two deliveries, the light deteriorated and we
had no option but to offer it to the Pakistani openers, who accepted our
offer and headed back to the pavilion. The difficulties for Merv and myself
came later when we decided to call play off for the day, with just these 2
balls making up the day's entertainment for the crowd. Refunds had been
available to the 8,500 ticket holders on the first day because there had been
no action but, as there had been some play, albeit a couple of balls, the
TCCB's regulations did not allow for the ticket holders to have any refunds.
Some of the spectators had paid upwards of £25 for their tickets, and were
very angry about the situation. Shortly after we called play off for the day,
a crowd of spectators gathered at the exit from the pavilion to vent their
frustration, so Merv and I had to be ushered out of a side door to avoid any
confrontation.

During the time that I was standing in Tests in England, all of the touring
sides had the opportunity of looking at the provisional panel of umpires
who the MCC had appointed for the Test matches when we stood in their
games against the county sides. This gave them the opportunity of giving
us the once over and, after they had sent in their report on our performance, we were either confirmed or replaced for the Test series. In 1988 I was
demoted from the Test panel after my poor performances during 1987 and,
as a consequence, I was not invited to umpire any of the matches involving

the West Indian tourists that summer. However, I redeemed myself in the county matches and finished high enough up the marking list at the end of the summer to earn a recall to the Test panel for 1989 and, for the next five years, I continued to stand in Tests, including a match in the 1989 Ashes series as well as the 1990 series with New Zealand, when I stood with Nigel Plews in a one-day international at Headingley, as well as the Third Test at Edgbaston with John Holder.

The West Indies were the visitors in 1991 for a five-Test series, and the TCCB appointed eight umpires to stand in the series – Dickie Bird, David Shepherd, Ken Palmer, John Hampshire, Mervyn Kitchen, Barry Dudleston, John Holder and myself. We all knew that it was going to be a particularly exciting season and one, given the tourists' fast bowlers, when we would be watching out for intimidatory bowling. But as we were all very experienced umpires, we did not foresee too many problems, especially as we had stood before in games involving the West Indies. This is precisely what happened when I stood in the Second Test at Lord's, when Robin Smith oversaw a recovery after England, in reply to the tourists' first innings total of 419, slipped to 84 for 5. Robin was playing superbly and, as the runs began to flow, the Caribbean bowlers started to get frustrated and peppered Robin with some short-pitched bowling. I was standing at the end that Curtly Ambrose was bowling from. Gradually his deliveries became more and more hostile with Robin, in his usual way, surviving this barrage of short stuff by watching the ball until, at the last split second, swaying out of the way. In one particular over, he began by sending two out of the first four balls fizzing past Robin's nose. I thought that two bouncers in an over were plenty and, as I wasn't prepared to let the situation continue, I simply said to Curtly, 'I'm counting those as the two for the over.' I expected Curtly to give a nod, or another form of acknowledgement, but he gave me no indication whatsoever and walked straight past me back to his mark. I thought that he had realised that he could risk a formal warning and that he would pitch the final two balls up. But the next ball was even quicker than the ones before it, and it shot past Robin's nose like a bullet. I didn't want to make a fuss, but I had to put a stop to this sort of bowling, which was clearly intimidatory, so I walked towards Curtly as he gathered the ball and headed back to take his mark. As we met, he put his arm around my shoulder and his face split into a wide grin. 'You're about to give me a real bollocking aren't you?' he said. I was speechless, and just nodded, before Curtly walked back and delivered the final ball, which was a normal delivery. Thankfully, for the rest of his spell Curtly resorted to more conventional means of taking wickets and he only used the bouncer as a surprise weapon, rather than a stock delivery clearly aimed at intimidating the batsman.

It was my turn to smile a bit later in the match as a fairly gusty wind started to blow, sending rubbish flying around the ground. As bits of paper started to cross the outfield, I couldn't help wondering how on earth Richie Richardson kept his well-known wide-brimmed floppy hat firmly on his head. As the gale continued, I wandered over to the West Indian and asked him what the secret was, to which Richie replied, 'Magic man, pure magic!'

THE ASHES AND THE HEADINGLEY TEST OF '81

Of the 26 Tests in which I stood, the most memorable was one of the greatest Tests of modern times – the Headingley Test of 1981 when Ian Botham's remarkable hitting and Bob Willis's bowling inspired England to a famous victory after they had followed-on against Australia. My partner in this amazing Test was David Evans, the former Glamorgan wicketkeeper who, incidentally, was standing in his first Test. Little did we think that the game would produce anything out of the ordinary as David and I, as per TCCB protocol, had a look at the wicket the day before the match started. We both noticed cracks in the wicket and agreed that whoever batted first would be at a huge advantage. Our assessment was validated as Australia, thanks to two brave innings from John Dyson and Kim Hughes, amassed 401 for 9 before bowling England out for 174 and inviting them to follow on. With wickets continuing to tumble in England's second innings on the Saturday evening, David and I even cancelled our accommodation for Monday evening in our guest house, fully expecting the game to be wrapped up on the fourth day.

But I.T. Botham had other ideas and, almost single-handedly, he turned the game on its head with one of the most destructive displays of hitting I was fortunate to witness in my umpiring career. He strolled to the crease in England's second innings with the scoreboard reading 105 for 5, with his side still needing a further 122 runs to avoid an innings defeat. I was standing at the bowler's end and can still recall his first shots. He began by slicing a drive over the slips, before driving behind square for another boundary. To his third ball, he made no contact with an airy drive, before nudging a single and jogging down to my end. As he arrived, I suggested to him that, in order for England to save the game, it might be a good idea to have a look for a while, to which 'Both' replied, 'But B.J., that's exactly what I've just done!'

The rest, of course, is history, as Ian proceeded to slaughter the bowling, hitting an unbeaten 149 and sharing an amazing eighth-wicket partnership of 117 with Graham Dilley that saw England wipe off the arrears and then accumulate a slender lead of 129. David Evans and I duly booked back into our guest house, still believing that Australia held the upper hand. But Ian's wonderful fightback had inspired his team and a fired-up Bob Willis then tore into the Australian batting, bowling from the Kirkstall Lane End at which David was standing. Bob took 8 for 43 as Australia collapsed in their second innings, making just 111 to give England a stunning 18-run victory. When the final wicket fell, a huge crowd swarmed onto the ground to mob their heroes and, as David and I walked off, they gathered in front of the Headingley pavilion singing and toasting England's success. It had been a thrilling match, and both David and I were quite drained as we sank into our chairs in the umpires' room. With the noise of the crowd filtering into our room, David and I didn't speak for a while as we just sat there, trying to take in what we had just witnessed. For David it had been a remarkable first Test and, after a few moments of reflection, he looked over at me and, with a grin on his face, said, 'Gosh B.J., I hope they're not all like that!'

There was, however, another reason why I remember the game, and that was because of a new TCCB ruling concerning extending the playing hours after interruptions for the weather. The TCCB had agreed to add an extra hour to the day's play when rain or bad light had led to playing time being lost, but the wording of their new playing condition was quite confusing, as we found out on the Saturday evening, when England followed on. With thick cloud hanging over the ground, there was a short delay right at the start of England's innings and then, after Graham Gooch was caught at slip off a beauty from Dennis Lillee, David and I offered the light again to England's batsmen, and we had another delay for over an hour before play began again with Australia's bowlers storming in fully refreshed after their break in the pavilion. Given the fact that we had been off for over an hour, it was announced that play would be extended for sixty minutes until 7 p.m., but the big black clouds were still hanging around and, with the light becoming very murky again, David and I offered the batsmen the light again and took the players off the field.

While in our umpires' room, we checked up again on the new playing conditions but, unfortunately, there was some misunderstanding over the wording, especially the phrase 'Should play be lost during the day, up to one hour could continue to be played at 6 p.m. providing play was still in progress.' David and I both interpreted this new clause as suggesting that we could only extend play if we were actually playing at 6 p.m., so at 5.55 p.m. we went outside with our light meters to see if the light had improved. It hadn't, so we summoned on the covers and told the two captains and the other officials that there would be no more play that day as the light was unfit.

Just as the announcements were being made over the public address system, the clouds cleared and the sun started to shine, leaving the crowd rather bemused about our decision. There was a lot of jeering and cushions were thrown in disgust, and a further announcement about why we had reached our decision did little to pacify the crowd, who believed that they had been short-changed. It was rather ironic that the very rule that the TCCB had brought in to give the public value for money should have caused this furore, but the problem was in the wording of the regulation and, shortly afterwards, the ruling was reworded, in crystal-clear language, that play could restart at any stage of the extra hour.

When the Aussies visited again in 1985 I stood with Ken Palmer in the opening match of the series that took place in mid-June at Headingley. In the lead-up to the match, there had been plenty of talk about the previous Ashes Test at Headingley, and the television footage of Ian Botham's heroics had received plenty of airings. My own memories of the epic match in 1981 came back as soon as I set foot in the umpires' room at the Leeds ground and, to the crowd's delight, there was a real-life repeat of the all-rounder's batting prowess as, in an hour of explosive hitting, Ian struck 60 off just 51 balls. As far as England were concerned, the heroes of this particular match were Tim Robinson – the Nottinghamshire opener, who made an impressive 175 and belied his reputation as a dour anchorman with a wide range of crisp strokes – and John Emburey, whose 5 for 82 in Australia's second innings, plus 4 wickets by Ian Botham, meant that England were left chasing 123 in a shade over three-and-a-quarter hours.

Despite the loss of 5 wickets, England eventually got home, but the end of the match, and the departure of Ken Palmer and myself from the field, was marred by a crowd invasion and subsequent melee in the middle that prompted David Gower to subsequently describe the behaviour of people who ran onto the pitch as being like 'a pack of mad dogs'. What made it even more unsavoury was that, three weeks before, in the European Cup

soccer final at Brussels, crowd unrest had led to the death of several spectators. Mindful of the possibility of a pitch invasion, the Yorkshire authorities
had made special announcements and a team of stewards was standing by
to help out. But with the scores level, and Allan Lamb hooking Simon
O'Donnell towards fine leg for the winning runs, the youths ran on. In
fact Geoff Lawson, who was fielding on the fine-leg boundary, made an
attempt to catch the ball but, with swarms of spectators running past him,
his chances of getting safely under the ball disappeared. Running back at
full tilt, he did well to lay a hand on the ball but, with the wave of intruders
swarming around him and disturbing his concentration, Geoff sank to the
ground in despair. As the mob approached, Kenny and I made an attempt to
gather the stumps and bails but, after a few skirmishes had taken place, we
left the youngsters – like a pack of hyenas with their prey – and, with the
help of a few stewards and policemen, we returned to the pavilion with a
semblance of dignity.

It was a very unfortunate ending to what had been a fine game of cricket.
The incident would have been even more alarming had England been 9
wickets down and, for the next few days, the papers were full of stories
about what would have happened if Geoff Lawson had needed to take the
catch in order to win the game. Several parallels were also drawn with some
of the ugly scenes on the football terraces, and some journalists even suggested that an answer to a repetition of this unsavoury event would be to
install high barbed-wire fences around the boundary edge. Thankfully, common sense and good behaviour has, by and large, prevailed and prevented
the cricket authorities from having to install such deterrents.

My next Ashes Test was the fourth game of the 1989 series at Old Trafford,
where I stood with John Hampshire, who was making his debut as a Test
umpire. Like many of the Tests that summer, the Aussies cruised to a comfortable win and, had it not been for a splendid rearguard action by Jack Russell
and John Emburey, the margin might have been by an innings, rather than
the eventual 9 wickets. As a 'member' of the Gloucestershire wicketkeepers'
union, it was quite pleasing for me to see Jack display his batting talents in
a Test arena. I knew from seeing him on the county circuit that he was a
more-than-capable left-handed batsman, and his unbeaten 128, compiled
during a five-and-three-quarter-hour stay at the crease, helped England
avoid an innings defeat. Events on the field, and the victory by Australia
that clinched the series, were rather overshadowed by news that emerged
during the Test that a party of sixteen English cricketers would be making a

three-month tour of South Africa, and the news of this so-called 'rebel' tour meant less space was given the following day on the cricket pages to the efforts of this fine Gloucestershire wicketkeeper at Old Trafford.

In 1993 I stood in two of the Ashes Tests – the Third Test at Trent Bridge with Roy Palmer, and the Sixth Test at The Oval with Merv Kitchen, which proved to be my final Test. The Australians, under Alan Border's captaincy, began the summer by winning at Old Trafford by 179 runs, followed by an innings victory at Lord's. So by the time Roy Palmer and I arrived in Nottingham to stand in the next Test, there were several changes to the England team. The selectors opted to inject some young blood into the team, giving Test debuts to twenty-one-year-old Mark Lathwell, twenty-three-year-old Graham Thorpe, twenty-four-year-old Martin McCague and twenty-two-year-old Mark Ilott. It was quite a baptism of fire for these youngsters, and there was plenty of intimidation in the intense atmosphere, with a lot of ribald comments directed at the batsmen. By the third evening, with England on 122 for 4 in their second innings, everyone's emotions were running so high that Roy and I felt it was time for action, and we reported the Australians for their bad language and also their questioning of our decisions, especially over bat-pad catches and lbws. Clive Lloyd, the match referee, concurred and reprimanded Allan Border's team. They were far more subdued after their censure from Clive, and centuries from Graham Gooch and debutant Graham Thorpe helped England to the safety of a draw.

After the Aussies had recorded another innings victory at Headingley, followed by a comfortable 8-wicket win at Edgbaston, I stood with Merv Kitchen in the final Test of the summer at The Oval. The outcome of the series had already been decided but, even so, the atmosphere was still very intense, and Allan Border's team were as keen as mustard to maintain the winning habit. As in the Test at Trent Bridge, the England selectors had made a number of changes from the previous Test and, for this game, Graeme Hick, Angus Fraser, Devon Malcolm, Mark Ramprakash and Steve Watkin were recalled to the team. In fact, it was Steve Watkin, the lion-hearted Glamorgan seamer, who was bowling when I made what were adjudged in the Press to be a couple of marginal decisions in England's favour. The first came early in Australia's second innings, as they chased 391 to win. Steve was bowling from my end to their opener Michael Slater and got one delivery to rise up sharply. It fizzed past the batsman at chest height and then, so I thought, deflected off his glove. Steve didn't really go up at first, but

Alec Stewart, the wicketkeeper, and all three of the England slip fielders immediately came running up towards the wicket, appealing for a catch. As Steve turned round to join in with the appeal, I raised my finger to give Slater out as I was quite convinced at the time that the ball had brushed his glove – it was only when I saw television replays from the reverse angle later that evening that I realised that the ball had in fact deflected off his armguard instead.

At the time I was unaware of the mistake I had inadvertently made and, as the happy fielders resumed their positions I gave David Boon, the next batsman, his guard. The next delivery was a huge in swinger from Steve Watkin, to which Boon padded up offering no stroke. Once again, I was convinced that the ball would have hit the stumps so I raised my finger again. I gather that some of the Press and television commentary team thought I had erred again, and believed that the batsman should have been given the benefit of the doubt. Later in the game, I gave a much more straightforward lbw decision against Shane Warne after Angus Fraser had rapped the leg-spinner on the pads right in front of the stumps. It meant too that England had won the game by 161 runs but, at 5.18 p.m. on 23 August 1993 it proved to be my final decision in Test cricket.

I hadn't had a happy game at The Oval, and the match at Trent Bridge had been a difficult one as well. After England's victory at The Oval, Merv and I shook hands with both teams and the other officials. We had a brief chat with some of the players, but I soon sensed that Allan Border had marked me poorly. Later that evening, when watching the highlights of the day's play on television, I realised my error with Slater's decision and, after all the events of the summer of 1993, I was not completely surprised when the TCCB subsequently informed me that I would not be on the international panel for 1994.

SEVEN

An Umpire's Lot

I believe that the umpire is on the field to help everyone to enjoy the game. I have enormous respect for the players who are out there to do their best and, in return, I expect them to respect my position. If I didn't think they did, then I would have stopped umpiring years ago. Being impartial is the main aim of any umpire, whether he or she is standing in a Test or a village match. During my time in the white coat, there were many occasions where, together with my colleague, I had some quite sensitive situations to deal with, and had to be seen to be fair to both sides. A case in point came quite early in my umpiring career, during the match towards the end of the 1974 season between Hampshire and Yorkshire on my 'home ground', Dean Park in Bournemouth.

With the destiny of the Championship title still in the balance, Hampshire had gone into the match with a slender 2-point lead over Worcestershire, who were playing Essex at Chelmsford. The weather interfered with both games, completely washing out play on the first day at Dean Park, while at Chelmsford there was a delayed start before Worcestershire bowled out Essex and gained maximum bowling points to leapfrog over Hampshire. But the rain then washed out the second day of the match at both Chelmsford and Bournemouth, and it was raining again when we got to the ground for the final day, with the Hampshire team itching to get into action and regain their place on top of the table. As the rain over Dean Park started to ease off, news filtered through from Essex that it was still raining heavily and that the match at Chelmsford was likely to be abandoned as a draw. As the rain clouds moved away from Bournemouth, Richard Gilliat, the Hampshire captain, became even more eager to play and he pushed Sam Cook and myself into thinking about a start. At the same time, the groundsman was throwing sawdust all over the square, while the pitch remained under cover but, after taking a look at the surrounds, Sam and I agreed that it was just not possible to make a start until the ground had dried up further.

As far as Yorkshire were concerned, they didn't really want to hang around and play for a couple of hours, as their next fixture was in Scarborough and, with a long car journey ahead of them, they wanted to get on the road as quickly as possible! But, with the rain having eased, Sam and I decided that, in order to be fair to all the counties concerned, we would wait and see if the ground could dry out a bit. We also asked the ground staff to remove the covers so that we could make sure that the wicket was fit. When it was uncovered the wicket was in a reasonable condition so, with the ground drying up, we decided to make a start. But, as soon as Sam and I walked out towards the middle, it started to spit with rain and, no sooner had we taken up our positions than the heavens opened, and the outfield was soon under-water again. We duly abandoned the game and, unfortunately for Hampshire, it meant they lost the Championship that weekend, as Worcestershire went on to clinch the title on the final day of the season.

As well as remaining impartial, an umpire has to have a full working knowledge of all the laws of the game, as well as an ability to quickly and correctly apply them given the various boundary markings at each ground. This is especially the case when catches are taken out in the deep, and the umpire has to instantly decide where the boundary lies relative to the fielder. The laws for catching are in any case quite complicated. I remember a game at Hove between Sussex and Middlesex when Kepler Wessels struck a fine double hundred, during which I had to adjudicate a boundary catch involving Mike Brearley. The Middlesex captain was fielding on the deep mid-wicket boundary but, in catching Wessels, he fell over the boundary line. Realising what was happening, Brearley tossed the ball back onto the field after taking the catch, believing that he had held the catch fairly. But I gave Wessels not out because Brearley had gone out of the field of play, even if the ball had not.

What is allowed is a fielder taking the catch inside the ropes and then, before he falls over, throwing it to another fielder who then completes the catch. If the fielder catches the ball in the field of play and then goes over the boundary still holding onto the ball, the batsman is accredited with a six. What complicates matters is the nature of the boundary – some grounds only have ropes demarcating the boundary, others have paint lines, sponsors boards or picket fences, while others have a combination of these and, before the start of each match, an umpire should familiarise themselves with the arrangements.

I can remember an incident when John Lever was playing for Essex and he was actually sitting on the fence at fine leg when he caught Steve Oldham off Norbert Philip's bowling. This was quite legitimate because, with a picket fence as the boundary, if any part of your body touches the ground on the other side of the fence or wall, then the catch is not legitimate. But if a fielder is leaning on, or as in John's case sitting on the fence, the catch is fair. You can also slide or run into the fence but, as long as you remain on the right side and still have the ball under control, the dismissal stands. However, some grounds have a combination of a rope inside a boundary fence or sponsor's board. If this is the case, the boundary is the rope, and diving or running across the rope and into the boards or fence while taking the catch means that the fielder is going outside the playing area, as in the case of Brearley above, and the catch cannot be given.

Being able to think quickly on your feet is another important attribute for an umpire – and not only when an appeal goes up, but when something unusual happens, as in a match in 1990 in my home town Bournemouth, involving Hampshire and Middlesex. Desmond Haynes and Mike Roseberry were batting for the visitors when Dessie took off his helmet, walked down the wicket and handed it over to Roseberry at the non-striker's end. I was a little bit bewildered and, going by instinct, I called over to Dessie and said, 'I don't think that you can do this.' 'Why not?' Dessie replied, to which I said, 'I don't know, but it doesn't look right and there is nowhere in the playing conditions that I can account for this issue. But supposing the ball hit your helmet while it was being held by Mike. I wouldn't know what to do, so please Dessie, I would ask you to be so kind as to replace your helmet.' With a smile on his face, Dessie duly put his helmet back on.

This is an example of the sort of thing that can crop up in a game where an umpire has to think quickly and carefully, and deal with a situation with a deft, human touch. It was the kind of situation for which there is nothing in the law book. As far as helmets are concerned, a fielder can place his helmet directly behind the wicket and if the ball, while in play, makes contact with it, the fielding team would incur a 5-run penalty. At the time, there was nothing about batsmen's helmets, except that they could call for them at any time. Umpires also need to have at their fingertips a complete understanding of all the playing regulations for each of the domestic competitions. While the laws of the game are always the same, each of the domestic competitions has its own playing conditions and, back in the 1970s and 1980s, the county calendar was very congested, with a variety of formats and competitions.

The three-day Championship matches usually started on Wednesdays, with the next game beginning on the Saturday, followed by a short break while the 40-overs a side John Player League match took place on the Sunday. But, at the start of the season, there was the 55-overs a side Benson & Hedges Cup, followed later in the season by the 60-overs a side Gillette Cup, as well as other limited-overs contests and friendlies against touring teams. In the days before the introduction of four-day games, the fixture list was certainly very hectic and congested and, from an umpire's point of view, it could also be quite confusing because of the subtle differences in each of the playing conditions. We had to stay on the ball, so I would also quickly check the regulations before each match to ensure that I wasn't caught out.

One of my most hectic periods came in July and August 1980 when I umpired six consecutive matches, each with different playing conditions. The sequence began on 16 July with a 60-over Gillette Cup match between Yorkshire and Kent at Headingley, followed on Saturday 19 July by the Benson & Hedges Cup final between Essex and Northants. But it rained on 19 July, and I had to drive up to Nottingham that night for the 40-over Sunday League match between Nottinghamshire and Worcestershire at Trent Bridge, before heading back down the M1 to London for the completion of the B&H final. My next game was the five-day Test match between England and the West Indies starting on 24 July and then, after a short break, I was back on duty at The Oval on 10 August for the three-day friendly between Surrey and Australia, which the latter were playing prior to the Centenary Test at Lord's. And then it was off to Derby for the three-day County Championship match between Derbyshire and Surrey.

In 1980 Scotland were added to the northern group for the zonal stage of the Benson & Hedges Cup. It meant that county teams and two umpires from England would wend their way up to Scotland and, besides the cricket, enjoy the hospitality that the generous Scots laid on, as well as, if time permitted, enjoying a round or two of golf on some of their fabulous courses. The only downside was that the B&H games were in late April or early May when, to be quite honest, the weather was not at its best. Terry Spencer and I were the two umpires for the first game in 1980, when Scotland made their competition debut by playing against Derbyshire at the Titwood ground in Glasgow. As I was living then in Derby, I made my way up with the county side to Crewe railway station, where we boarded an express for Glasgow.

It was quite a long journey so in 1988, when Jack Birkenshaw and I were appointed for the match against Leicestershire, we jumped at the chance to join the English county on their specially chartered plane from the East Midlands airport. It was a quicker journey, but only just, as we had to circle over Glasgow for around an hour because the airport's runway was blocked by an Irish plane that had landed poorly in the bad weather. The storm was still blowing when we eventually landed, and it kept going for the next two days, forcing the match to be abandoned without a ball being bowled.

The game in 1980 turned out to be a comfortable 10-wicket victory for Derbyshire on a pitch and outfield that weren't all that grand, and in bitterly cold weather. In fact, I had to wear so many layers of clothing that I could barely get my white coat on! In addition to my usual attire – singlet and pants, a long-sleeved thermal vest, long john thermal underwear, white shirt and tie, trousers, socks, boots and sleeveless cricket sweater – I wore a long-sleeved cricket sweater with my golfing jacket, and then on top of that my white coat, but only just!

The TCCB were very generous at the beginning of each season, because they gave us coats of two different sizes – a longer one for the cooler, early season weather, and a shorter and thinner one for when the weather improved. However, none of this gear assisted in keeping our hands warm. Whereas the players had plenty of time to move around and keep their circulation going, we poor umpires did not move around much, and some-times our fingers became so stiff with cold that it was difficult to move the counters from one pocket to another to count the balls in the over. I tried wearing all types of gloves – leather, surgical and ordinary woollen ones, but it's not very convenient to have one's hands encased when trying to write down on our cards the number of overs against each bowler, or when putting bails on or off, so I just had to grin and bear it.

There have also been changes in the technical gadgets that we, as umpires, had to take onto the field. The 1978 season saw the introduction of light meters by the TCCB. In the early days it was quite a compact device, with a needle moving from point 0 to point 10, which would give us an indication of whether the light had deteriorated or not. However, there was nothing in the playing conditions, or the laws of cricket, to tell us when, and if, the meter should be used. Their introduction was to provide an objective read-ing and a guide that proved to both the crowd and players that the light had deteriorated. Previously we had been reliant on the human eye, and had to take into consideration who was bowling, the type of background and whether it had become too dangerous to continue. Their use in 1978 was initially on a trial basis and, although I conferred with my colleague with the meter, I still liked to rely on the human eye and my instinct. If we felt that we would offer the light to the batsmen, we then had a meter reading that we could use to compare with later situations if we came out later on to see if the light had improved. They also helped us if the batsman decided not to accept the offer of bad light, and decided to continue batting. We could still take a reading and put it in lock and, if there was a subsequent appeal thereafter, we were able to use the initial reading as a guideline. I felt overall that it was a great asset and, even when I retired in 1997, there was still nothing in the law book or in the playing conditions about its use. It was clear that the powers-that-be viewed it as an aid, rather than something that took away an umpire's authority.

Many changes have also taken place during my cricket career in what I would call 'cricket etiquette'. Players nowadays pressurise umpires more than ever before, and the umpire gets little help from the players when it comes to making the right decision. Now I'm not saying that this is right or wrong but, in the past, many batsmen would walk as soon as they got a faint edge on the ball, often heading back to the pavilion before the umpire had even raised his finger. By the 1980s and 1990s many players remained at the crease while the appeal took place, believing that it is the umpire's job to give them either out or not out. This can, on occasions, lead to a bit of gamesmanship, with batsmen rubbing their forearms or fielders going into a congratulatory huddle.

I had come straight from playing into umpiring at a time when most players were prepared to walk off, even before a decision was made. Back in the 1960s and 1970s, there was little money about and no sponsors. Nowadays, players are well-paid and sponsored, but I still don't see why many of them should react the way they do, except, I suppose, that results are more important to them because of the financial rewards. There were sometimes other reasons why modern batsmen would hang around at the crease awaiting a decision, as I found out in the 1980 Lord's Test between England and the West Indies. Alvin Kallicharran got what I felt to be a straightforward edge to a ball from Bob Willis and was caught by Alan Knott. As was my usual custom, I duly raised my finger and called, 'That's out.' On this particular occasion, Alvin had completely turned away from me as the appeal was made, so I assumed he had clearly not heard me the first time. I gave him out for a second time, and also called out, 'Kalli – I've given you out caught behind.'

1. *Above left:* Kenneth and Barrie Meyer.

2. *Above right:* Barrie and his parents.

3. Young B.J.

4. *Above left:* A very young B.J.

5 *Above right:* Young Barrie on Boscombe beach.

6. *Below:* Barrie and his bike.

7. *Above:* St Clements Junior School 1942/43. Barrie is in the centre of the front row.

8. *Right:* The Boscombe Secondary School six-a-side football team, with Barrie holding the trophy.

9. The Boscombe Secondary School team – cup winners 1945/46 – with Mr Hawthorne (teacher).

10. *Opposite above:* The Pokesdown Lads football team.

11. *Opposite below:* The Hampshire Boys' Club team for the 1949/50 season.

12. *Right:* Barrie proudly wearing his England schoolboy cap.

13. *Below:* The England Schoolboys team of 1948/49

14 Barrie and the Bristol Rovers team of 1954/55. From left to right, back row: Peter Sampson, Harry Bamford, Howard Radford, Frank Allcock, Paddy Hale. Front row: Dai Ward, George Petherbridge, Jack Pitt, Geoff Bradford, Barrie Meyer, Peter Hooper.

16. Barrie Meyer challenges Bristol City goalkeeper Bob Anderson in the FA Cup fifth-round tie in 1958, which Bristol Rovers won 4-3.

15. *Opposite below:* Barrie at Eastville after joining Bristol Rovers.

17. Fred Titmus pulls a ball from John Mortimore during Middlesex's innings against Gloucestershire at Lord's in September 1961. Barrie is behind the stumps, with Arthur Milton at slip.

18. Barrie attempts to run out Middlesex's Ron Hooker in the County Championship match at Lord's in August 1963.

19. Barrie plays a ball against Middlesex's Alan Moss in August 1963.

20. Barrie is bowled by Don Bennett – another footballer/cricketer – during the Championship encounter between Middlesex and Gloucestershire in May 1964.

21. Barrie keeping wicket against the 1964 Australians.

22. E.A. Clark hits out against the bowling of Tony Windows as Middlesex play Gloucestershire in June 1965.

23. *Above:* Barrie attempts to run out Middlesexs' Eric Russell in June 1965.

24. *Below:* The Gloucestershire XI with the Duke of Beaufort in 1967. From left to right, back row: Tony Windows, Syd Russell, Mike Bissex, Tony Brown, Barrie Meyer, David Brown. Front row: Ron Nicholls, David Allen, John Mortimore, Arthur Milton and David Smith.

25. *Opposite:* Dickie.

26. *Right:* Barrie with fellow Test umpire John Holder at Archdeacon Meadow, Gloucester in May 1995.

27. *Below:* HRH Prince Andrew meets umpires Barrie Meyer, John Hampshire and Barrie Leadbeater at the Old Trafford Test in 1989.

Three great players from Barrie's umpiring days.

28. *Above:* Ian Botham.

29. *Left:* Alvin Kallicharran.

30. *Opposite:* Clive Lloyd.

31 & 32. The final match – Gloucestershire *v.* Lancashire, September 1997.

This time, he turned around and I said, 'I'm not going to give you out again' before he walked off. At the close of play, I popped along with my towel to the shower room – in those days, we had to share facilities with the players – and lo and behold, but there was Alvin still standing there, cooling off. I said to him, 'Kalli – why did you stand on me today? You knew that you were out.' He agreed with me, but added that, as he was short of runs, he thought that he might get away with it. We smiled at each other, and that was the end of the episode.

I'm glad to say that this was an isolated incident and if a player had over-stepped the mark and got their etiquette badly wrong with an umpire, they were usually quite ready to apologise, albeit in private in the umpires' room. A case in point came at Edgbaston in July 1990 during the Test between England and New Zealand after I had given Martin Crowe, the fine Kiwi batsman, out lbw to Chris Lewis. The England all-rounder had trapped him right in front of the stumps but, believing that the ball was missing the stumps, Crowe had turned his back on me as I lifted my finger for the first time. Unaware of my decision, Crowe remained at the crease with his back to me, so I had to call to him to say that I had already given him out and, as he turned around, I lifted my finger for a second time. He walked off rather despondently but then, during the next interval, Crowe came to the umpires' room and immediately apologised to me for his behaviour and for questioning my decision. He said that it was very unprofessional of him and he assured me that it would not happen again. I accepted his apology and said that the matter was closed as far as I was concerned. Unfortunately though for Martin, he was lbw again in the second innings after he had been hit on his pads by Devon Malcolm. I had to give him out for a second time in the match, but this time he walked off without a murmur.

A batsman walking for an lbw is, of course, a very rare event, but this is precisely what happened in 1980 during the Test at Old Trafford when Desmond Haynes, on 184, walked after being rapped on the pads by Ian Botham. I hadn't even raised my finger when Desmond headed off to the pavilion – he was a fine batsman and, as this example shows, a gentleman as well. Coincidentally, I also officiated when he made 220 for Middlesex at Ilford in June 1990, and later that season when he also scored 255 not out against Sussex at Lord's. As we shared a small drink after his innings at Lord's, we spoke about these three fine innings, and Desmond said to me, 'Well, B.J., I think you are my good luck omen – would you be able to accompany me in the winter when the West Indies are touring Australia?'

Another trend that increased during my umpiring career was for fielding teams actually appealing for a decision – whether it was caught behind, a bat and pad catch or for leg before – knowing perfectly well that the appeal is unwarranted. I experienced this on an increasing number of occasions. An example was the decision I mentioned earlier in my final Test match when I gave Michael Slater out caught behind in August 1993, when England were playing Australia at The Oval. At the time, I was quite convinced that the ball had brushed Slater's glove, and it was only later that evening, when I was watching the television replays from behind the wicket, that I realised from this reverse angle that Slater had not in fact gloved the ball, and that the ball had actually deflected from his arm guard. Everyone behind the wicket could see this, and the England fielders were well aware of this, yet Alec Stewart the wicketkeeper and the three slips still came running towards me, appealing for a catch.

These appeals are now commonplace in modern cricket. To my mind, the players making the appeals are behaving in a manner that contravenes the phrase 'spirit of cricket' in law 42, and I'm so pleased that in county cricket there has been a recent change to introduce a 'Spirit of Cricket Award', with the umpires marking each of the Championship teams. I hope that this encourages the players to do something about appealing, and return to the days of genuine appeals – though even this might be too much to ask for when there is so much money at stake in the modern game, and when there is promotion and relegation possible.

Splitting the Championship into two is yet another change in the game, adding an extra dimension to matches that, in my day, were simply about gaining bonus points and, at the end of the year, a final position out of seventeen. Avoiding relegation or gaining promotion has added both an extra cut and thrust to proceedings, and a new source of conflict and incident – all adding to the umpire's lot.

Bouncers, Poor Wickets and a Certain Jack Russell

Regular bouncers and nasty rising balls just short of a length became commonplace in Test match cricket from the 1970s onwards, giving the Press much to write and talk about. I had several occasions when I had to deal with persistent short-pitched deliveries, including the Test match at Lord's in June 1980 between England and the West Indies. Bob Willis – the

Warwickshire paceman – was the bowler in question, having returned from the winter tour to Australia without much success. But on this day at Lord's Bob was firing on all cylinders and bowling with some real pace and fire. Facing Willis was Colin Croft, normally the West Indian number ten or eleven but, on this occasion, he had been promoted to nightwatchman, and was now batting at number three. As far as I was concerned, his promotion meant that he would be expected to deal with short-pitched bowling – had he been in his normal position, then it would have been a different matter, and we would not have tolerated any short-pitched balls.

Bob was firing pretty well from my end, and he unleashed one very straight and quick bouncer that fizzed past Croft's nose. Willis then bowled another short and straight bouncer and Croft got out of the way, but only just. I felt that two successive bouncers was overstepping the mark and unacceptable. There were no stipulations at the time regarding the number of bouncers per over, or intimidatory bowling, and we only had Law 42 and the phrase 'spirit of cricket' to work with. But, after seeing the way Croft had scrambled out of the way of Willis's second successive bouncer, I felt that I had to act, especially as the situation looked as if it might get out of hand unless something was done.

I called over Ian Botham, the England captain, and spoke to him briefly, before consulting my colleague Bill Alley and calling over Willis to warn him that I was acting under law 42. Botham was quite understanding and Willis completed his over, before heading down to long-leg where he came in for a battery of abuse from some of the West Indian supporters. He reacted by gesturing to the crowd and, from where I was standing, I thought he had gone over the mark. Botham assured me that this was not the case, and that he was only jesting and having a bit of banter with the crowd, so I let the matter rest. Willis proceeded to bowl more orthodox deliveries to Croft before the nightwatchman was run out. I thought that that was the end of the matter, but I later read the report of the correspondent of the *News of the World* who said that my intervention had seemed premature, particularly as there had been no agreement between the captains about the number of bouncers. I felt that the fact that the captains had not reached an agreement to be totally irrelevant – the important thing in my mind was for the bowler to be completely, and quickly, aware of what is acceptable and what is not.

During my time in the game, there have been several occasions when doubt has been cast over the legality of a bowler's action. My mind immediately goes back to the 1960s when bowlers such as Tony Lock of Surrey and England and Harold Rhodes of Derbyshire and England were called for throwing, while in 1960 Geoff Griffin, the Springbok fast bowler, was called twenty-eight times for 'chucking' during the South Africans' tour of England. The umpires concerned in these matches were acting under law 24, number 2, which stated that 'The umpire has the right to call "no ball" if he is not satisfied with the absolute fairness of the delivery. For the delivery to be fair, the ball must be bowled, not thrown. If either umpire is not entirely satisfied with the fairness of a delivery, then he should call "no ball" instantly upon delivery.'

Rather than calling a bowler immediately, I preferred the 'softly softly' route. If I had doubts about someone's action, I would speak to their captain at the end of the day or would talk to the bowler himself, saying that I was not completely satisfied with their method of delivery. If I still felt that something was not right, I would make a report to Lord's and, after an investigation, they would deal with the matter as they saw fit, often using television videos or film from sideways on. It is, though, quite difficult for an umpire to assess a bowler's action and be absolutely sure that he has thrown a delivery, especially when standing at the bowler's end, as you can't watch his arm that closely if at the same time you are watching his feet to see if he's no-balling. Nowadays we have more improved technical tools to help us assess the legality or otherwise of actions, and an umpire is putting his own career, and also that of the bowler in jeopardy, by making a snap decision out on the field. A case in point relates to Muttiah Muralitharan, the Sri Lankan spinner, who had been taken to task by many umpires, before being called in 1999 by umpire Darrell Hair from Australia. Quite a controversy arose, as the Sri Lankan captain duly led his team off the field because he objected to Hair's call. The ICC have subsequently studied in considerable detail Muralitharan's method of delivery, and after much studying of the evidence his action has been cleared and deemed acceptable.

In my view, an umpire who calls a bowler after all of this evidence is asking for controversy, and the correct way to sort out the matter would be for the umpire to have a quiet word with the bowler and his captain. If need be the bowler can be reported to the authorities, and any controversy can then be resolved by a committee using modern technology. A calm decision after careful deliberation, instead of a decision made in the heat of the moment, could go a long way towards clarifying bowling actions.

In 1981 a change took place to the regulations regarding pitch covering, with the TCCB deciding that the whole pitch and the surrounding areas should be covered. Before then only the two ends of the pitch had been covered, with the rest of the wicket, and the bowler's run-ups, open to the elements. I had been brought up on uncovered wickets and, throughout my playing career, there were times when the vagaries of the English weather made it difficult to get play under way. I can still remember one year when Gloucestershire travelled up to Old Trafford and then on to Leicester, and spent all six days cooped up in the pavilion. And there was a game at Edgbaston when we were playing Warwickshire on a damp surface, and Martin Young, our opening batsman, came back into our dressing room, and removed his pads that were covered in muddy splash marks! There was also an occasion when all six days of the Gloucester Festival were badly affected by the weather and, by the 1980s, when county cricket was becoming more of a commercial undertaking, this wasn't good enough as far as spectators and sponsors were concerned, and covering the wickets meant that they could see more cricket. Covering the wickets was also for the best as far as the players were concerned, because it made each surface true and a much fairer test between bat and ball, compared with the days of uncovered wickets. And, as a long-standing member of the wicketkeepers' union, I have to add that it wasn't only the batsmen who were helped as, many a time on a damp wicket, I found it extremely difficult to keep to the likes of John Mortimore or David Allen on a wicket where the ball was lifting and spinning sharply. Through no real fault on my part, the ball would fizz off the damp surface and shoot over my left shoulder for byes! The changes in 1981 have therefore produced better pitches, more chance of play and, as soon as the rain has stopped, the groundsmen can get out to the middle and start to mop up and get the ground ready for play, reducing the feelings of frustration for the players or spectators.

Despite the changes in these regulations, there were still occasions when I encountered substandard wickets – the most notorious occasion being in August 1989 when Nottinghamshire played Derbyshire in the County Championship at Trent Bridge. I was standing with Peter Wight, the former Somerset and West Indian batsman and, when we inspected the wicket before play, we found it was worn and not in very good condition. There was nothing that we could do about things until the game started though. In no time at all, it was obvious that the match was not going to go the distance. Michael Holding, the great West Indian fast bowler, was bowling length balls that were rearing up and hitting Chris Broad, the Nottinghamshire and England opener, on the chest and arm. Chris bravely saw things through to

get 57 as Nottinghamshire made 185, with off-spinner Reg Sharma also
getting assistance from one of the worn ends to take 4 for 31. Derbyshire
then mustered 165, with their captain Kim Barnett making a splendid 80
in ninety-five minutes as West Indian quick bowler Franklyn Stephenson
got lift and venomous bounce at one end, and Eddie Hemmings's off-spin
turned sharply at the other. Derbyshire's first innings ended just before the
close on the Saturday night, but Peter Wight and myself had already reported
the pitch to the TCCB as, after what we had witnessed in the morning session, I had contacted Lord's during the lunch break. Things did not get
any better when Nottinghamshire batted again on the Monday morning,
with their opening batsmen, Chris Broad and Paul Pollard, being hit several
times by the Derbyshire fast bowlers Michael Holding and Devon Malcolm.
Chris vented his displeasure by making several gestures with his bat, including pointing his bat in the direction of the Trent Bridge groundsman, Ron
Allsop, who was standing near the boundary rope and then, when he was
dismissed by Holding, he shook hands with the Nottinghamshire fielder
who had caught him. It was clear that something needed to be done so,
soon afterwards, I summoned the two captains – Tim Robinson and Kim
Barnett – and explained to them that neither Peter nor myself were satisfied with the state of the pitch, and that we felt it was too dangerous for the
players to continue.

Tim and Kim agreed with our decision, so we took the players off the
field, and I immediately went into the secretary's office and, after explain-
ing things to the Nottinghamshire secretary, I made an announcement over
the public address system so that the spectators were kept informed. Then
I contacted Lord's again to both explain what had happened that morning
and also to ask for a decision about what should happen next.

After a delay, a statement came from the TCCB office to say that the
match should resume if it was possible to prepare another pitch, and added
Donald Carr and Tim Lamb would soon be on their way from Lord's to
inspect the wicket. With the Fifth Test having finished the previous week
on an adjoining wicket, both captains agreed to switch over onto this used
surface, although Michael Holding disagreed and decided to take no further
part in the match. This was, of course, no concern of the umpires, and it was
a matter for Derbyshire and their captain to resolve.

The Press, who, from the action on Saturday, were well aware of the situation, knew that there were some good stories to be written, and my good
friend Michael Carey of *The Independent*, got confirmation of our decision

to take the players off when he spoke to Bernie Maher. The Derbyshire wicketkeeper said immediately to Michael, 'It is now quicker than on the first day, and if we had continued there was a definite possibility of someone getting killed.'

After a delay of two hours, the game finally resumed, although things were still far from ideal on a surface that had already been played on for five days, and had only been briefly rolled and cut on the Monday morning. While the surface was very loose and under-prepared, at least it wasn't dangerous, but the spinners then had a field day as Barnett took 4 for 36 as the home team were dismissed for 114, before Hemmings snaffled 5 for 20 as Derbyshire were bowled out for 64 to give Nottinghamshire a 70-run victory.

Soon after the end of the game, Messrs Carr and Lamb arrived from Lord's to see things for themselves, and the three-man panel the TCCB conveyed also came to the same conclusion, with the outcome being that Nottinghamshire were fined 25 points for preparing an unsatisfactory wicket. Their statement duly said the pitch 'was clearly under-prepared and undoubtedly unfit for first-class cricket. In reaching their conclusion, the panel took into consideration the difficulties facing the groundsman due to the long, hot spell and noted Nottinghamshire's comment regarding the shortage of preparation time due to the preceding Test Match. The panel stressed there was no question of any deliberate intent or malpractice.'

But my time as an umpire in county and international cricket was not all about controversy and difficult decisions, and there were a host of funny little incidents, both on and off the field, that brought a smile to my face. Some of these were quite private, and unheard by the crowd. An example came in a Sunday League match at Hull in 1981 involving Yorkshire and Glamorgan. My colleague was another former member of the wicketkeepers' union, Peter Eele, the former Somerset gloveman. Glamorgan had made 153 for 8 in an innings that, because of rain, was reduced to 38 overs. When Yorkshire batted, John Hampshire was run out for 2, and then Jim Love was dismissed by the final ball of an over for 8. The next batsman in was Kevin Sharp and, as the previous over had been completed, he walked in to stand by me at the non-striker's end. Bill Athey was on strike for the next over and, to the first delivery, he firmly drove the ball straight back towards the bowler, who managed to just get a fingertip to it, and deflect the ball onto the stumps at my end. The wicket was broken with Kevin well out of his ground as he backed up, and I duly raised my finger to give Kevin run out.

After the match, I had a chat with Kevin and said, 'Bad luck, Sharpie – that was a terrible way to get out.' He replied that he had just been talking to one of the Yorkshire statisticians, who had told him that he had just equalled the record for the number of noughts in Sunday League games. I said, 'Gee, that must be some sort of record – who was the other player involved?' to which his reply was 'You!'

Another funny thing happened to me once when I was driving south through Hampshire to stand the next day in a Championship match at Southampton. After spending a lot of time on the motorway, I decided to head off onto the back roads and travel the last leg of the journey via a more scenic route. I had headed through the pretty countryside for several miles when I had a blow-out in one of my tyres. I pulled into the next lay-by, jumped out of my car and started to change the wheel. After a few minutes, I was conscious that there were one or two curious faces behind me, watching what I was doing. I then spotted a metal plate on a gatepost in the lay-by that informed me that I was outside a mental institution.

With my audience watching every move, I proceeded quickly to change the wheel by taking off the hubcap and unscrewing the four nuts that held the wheel in place. I then placed the hubcap onto the pavement with the four screws resting on top, so that I did not misplace any of these screws. However, in taking off the final hubcap, I knocked one of the other ones on the pavement and, to my horror, the four screws ran into an adjoining drain. After muttering a few oaths under my breath, I took off my jacket, rolled up my sleeve and put my hand down the drain in the hope of finding the screws. As I frantically moved my hand and arm around in the drain, one of the inmates then called out to me. 'Looks like you've got a bit of trouble there sport,' he said. 'I think the only thing you can do now is to take one nut from each of the other three wheels, then you'll have three nuts on each wheel, and that should be enough to get you back to a place where you can find a garage.'

I thought about this helpful advice and, realising it was quite useful, I duly got out my spare tyre, replaced each wheel with three screws, put the punctured tyre into the boot and slammed the boot shut. Before getting back into the car, I turned to my advisor and said, 'Thank you very much for your help, sir.' He replied, 'You're most welcome', to which I said, 'What puzzles me is why an intelligent chap like you is staying in a place where you are.' He said, 'Well sir, I'm a sex maniac, not a bloody idiot.'

However, other funny incidents were far more public, such as the one that took place quite early during my umpiring career in the televised John Player Sunday League match at Edgbaston in 1975, and it wasn't until after the game that I was fully aware of precisely what had happened. The match in question involved Warwickshire and Kent and, after a slightly delayed start, the contest got underway as a 37-overs a side match. Kent batted first and made 140 for 6, and Warwickshire's reply was going quite well until they had a mini-collapse, which meant they needed 8 runs to win off the final over. As the over was about to begin, my colleague Don Oslear came over to speak to me, because a small group of four youths had jumped over the boundary fence and were sitting along the boundary rope at the far end of the ground. They were not too far away from Asif Iqbal, one of the Kent fielders, and it was clear from the noise that the lads were making that they had been drinking for most of the afternoon.

My first thought was to leave well alone as we only had 6 balls remaining, but Don was concerned that a ball might go in their direction and that this could lead to problems. The game was an important one for both sides, so we decided to wander over in their direction so that the police or the stewards could move them back outside the boundary fence in order to avoid any possible unpleasantness. So Don and I set off in a purposeful manner over towards the rowdy youths and, as we got towards them, the crowd started to roar with laughter. Don and I looked at each other because we could not find anything remotely funny about the incident and, to make matters worse, we couldn't see a steward in the area, and realised that we would have to speak with the group.

However, as we got closer to them, they decided that discretion was the better part of valour and jumped back over the fence. Don and I therefore turned around and headed back to our positions. As the match resumed, there were still some smiles on the faces of the Kent fielders, and a few ripples of laughter were still going around the home spectators, but these soon stopped as, with the first ball of the final over, Derek Underwood got Steve Rouse out leg-before. The equation now was 8 to win off 5 balls, and in strode Eddie Hemmings to become the hero of the hour, by striking the fourth and fifth balls to the boundary to set up a 2-wicket victory for his team.

As I drove back after the game, I was still wondering what all the laughter was about. I was quite keen to get home so, after having a shower and a quick drink, I jumped straight into my car and headed off. As soon as I got home, my wife said that she had been watching, and she said that she had particularly liked the funny incident before the start of the final over. I immediately replied that, as far as I had been concerned, it hadn't been humorous at all, especially as it had been an extremely tense match. My wife just smiled back, and then explained why there had been such a roar of mirth from the crowd as Don and I had marched over to deal with the youths. A Jack Russell terrier had run out from the crowd, raced out to the middle and, after nosing around for a while, had cocked its leg against one of the stumps! I've heard of watering the wicket, but this takes the biscuit – perhaps the dog biscuit!

What they said about B.J.

Frank Keating on Barrie Meyer and David Evans
standing in the Lord's Test of 1984 (from *The Guardian*, 30 June 1984)

The throng at this old and legendary sporting arena are blessed with light, sweetness and serenity. Players in white chivalrously honour the foe – they smile among each other, and come and go with no demonstration of defiance or demure.

They are under the supervision of two quiet, calm and calming men, both in their early fifties with honest, level-gazed, watery-bright eyes and hale, nut-brown countrymen's faces. For six hours a day they stand, unnoticed, almost anonymous, yet in a way directing, orchestrating the drama itself.

Like sentries they stand, never suspicious, but ever ready. Hands behind their back, or in their pockets as they notch off the minutes and deliveries with their counting tools of barrels and coins, plodding in from square-leg and out again, and in again, always watching, always waiting, always prepared.

On the eve of the match, I walked up the hotel staircase with our undynamic duo. Bob Willis strolled over to say hello. Now we bumped into other players – 'Oh gosh! Got you again, have we?' says David Gower to Meyer with touching friendliness. Ian Botham then greets Evans with, 'Yachi da, boyo,' and puts his great paw on the umpire's shoulder in welcome. As we walk on, Evans says, 'Oh, he's a good boy Ian,' and Meyer adds, 'Yes, never any trouble with him is there!?'

EIGHT

Winter Work

Being a first-class umpire with the TCCB meant that I had guaranteed work, and a reasonable salary, between the months of April and September. As far as the rest of the year was concerned it was up to me and, with a wife and family to support, I still needed something to help me through the winter months.

Modern county cricketers are very fortunate – they are well paid for their summer work with the counties, and there are plenty of other jobs to be had with county clubs or coaching overseas. Some counties even employ their contracted players for twelve months a year but, back in the 1960s, every county, including Gloucestershire, only gave contracts for the summer months.

Finding winter work had never been too much of a problem earlier in my playing career with Gloucestershire, but my life as a professional footballer with League clubs had drawn to an end in the early 1960s. Towards the end of the 1962/63 season, Fred Ford, the Bristol City manager, had made it clear that I had only been signed as cover for the established first-team players. In the spring of 1963 my thoughts had started to turn to cricket, but then I received a call from Roy Daniel, the former Arsenal and Wales footballer, who was player-manager at Hereford United. We subsequently met up and he offered me £20 per week, plus expenses, provided that I could find the time to train twice a week at Hereford. Roy was very persuasive and, in July 1963, I agreed terms with him. Soon after travelling to the Edgar Road ground, I realised how serious and committed they were. Don Bennett, the Middlesex cricketer who had played for Arsenal and Coventry, was also on their books, together with Bill Holden, the former Burnley player and Bill Parry, who had played for Blackpool in an FA Cup final. They were a very

nice bunch of lads to train with but, to be honest, I didn't really enjoy playing
for Hereford, and the following winter I had no hesitation in accepting an
offer to travel to South Africa where I worked at the Union High school at
Graaf Reinet – a small farming town in Cape Province, some 170 miles or
so north of Port Elizabeth. The co-educational school had around 250 boys,
most of whom were mad keen on sport. For several years they had employed
an English county professional and, originally, David Brown of Warwickshire
had been invited to be their coach for the 1964/65 season. But David was
chosen for the MCC winter tour, and I was asked if I would like to do the
job instead. With my football-playing career seemingly coming to an end,
it didn't take me long to say yes to their offer. In previous years they had
employed Syd Buller, the former Test umpire, and Warwickshire's Freddie
Gardner and Basil Bridge. It didn't take me long to appreciate their influence,
as we easily beat several schools of similar size who did not employ county
coaches. My duties involved around eighteen hours each week of coaching
in the nets and, whenever there were games, I was asked to umpire. As most
fixtures were on Saturday afternoons, it meant that I had little spare time at
weekends, and only got the chance to play in a couple of games. However, I
did get six weeks off over the Christmas period, and I travelled to Cape Town
to spend the time with my Gloucestershire colleague Martin Young. Being
in Cape Town also meant that I could watch the Test between South Africa
and England at the Newlands ground. Temperatures at times soared to 114°F
– the first time I had ever spent Christmas in such heat.

I really enjoyed myself in South Africa in the winter of 1964/65; so much
so that I agreed to return the following year with my wife Gillian to coach
at St Andrews College in Grahamstown. It was another winter of coaching,
umpiring and helping out in the nets, as well as passing on the odd bit of
advice to the club and provincial players who frequented the nets. Jimmy
Crossan – the chairman of the Port Elizabeth City Football Club, who had
just entered the South African National League – also approached me. He
asked me if I wanted to be player-manager of the club, who were equivalent
to a good Southern League club. I watched them play a couple of times,
and I realised that interest was growing in the sport. However, I wasn't really
interested in their offer as the South African soccer season coincided with
the English county season. It would have meant giving up playing county
cricket and I was not prepared to do that.

Gillian was quite keen to settle down back home, so we returned to Britain
in the spring of 1966, with me looking forward to the new season with

Gloucestershire, and hoping to find something over the winter months. As luck would have it, shortly after my return, I had a phone call from George Petherbridge, one of my old football pals with Bristol Rovers. George was now the manager of Glastonbury FC, who played in the Western League, and he asked if I was interested in joining his club. At first I told him that I was not really very interested in playing non-League football, but he wouldn't take no for an answer, and he continued to ring me up. George's badgering resulted in me agreeing in September 1966 to sign on for Glastonbury at the princely sum of £5 per game. At first, it was quite odd being back in the Western League almost twenty years after playing as a youngster with Bristol Rovers Colts. There were several quite wily old players playing for the various clubs in the league who would not think twice about making a fool of a former Football League professional. But I gradually found my feet, the goals started to pop in and, in the 1967/68 season, I was Glastonbury's leading scorer with 14 goals.

What they said about B.J.

George Petherbridge – Bristol Rovers (1946-1962)
and later manager of Glastonbury

I was really delighted when Barrie agreed to play for us. I knew from my Bristol Rovers days what a fine all-round footballer he was. He excelled at everything he did, and he was such a nice bloke as well.

After joining us, Barrie slotted in immediately. There were no airs and graces with him, and he never boasted to others about his League career or great days with the Rovers. He fitted in right from day one and was so enthusiastic.

I was sorry to see him leave Glastonbury, but I knew it was right for him, and that he was destined for greater things with cricket.

It was nice to play football once again, but my limbs were starting to ache and, the following winter, I decided to hang my boots up once and for all and to look for alternative work over the winter months. At first I was lucky enough to secure a position with a company based in Leeds who sold fireworks and Christmas cards. They already employed three other cricketers – Derbyshire's Bob Taylor and David Smith, as well as Bob White of Middlesex and Nottinghamshire, so there were a few familiar faces around, but my sales area seemed to stretch from Cornwall to Scotland, and I spent a lot of time on the road. After this, I mixed my winters for a while selling fire extinguishers for a company called Nu-swift, and playing golf. Like many other county cricketers, I really like to have a round of golf – it's another great game, and I found it a great way to relax as well as keeping fit over the winter months. It's a wonderful way of blowing the cobwebs away, and also filling in time between and after matches, as well as on days when the weather has prevented any play from taking place. When I was standing in Tests, the Sunday was a rest day so, more often than not, I would spend my free time on the fairways of a local club, often with some of the players and members of the media covering the Test. It was really something to get onto a course surrounded by beautiful scenery, to pit your wits against plenty of water hazards, and spend the afternoon in good company, while at the same time concentrating on 'chasing the ball'.

Several of my umpiring colleagues were also fine golfers, especially the late Chris Balderstone. Chris and I were pretty well matched as far as golfing prowess was concerned, and we enjoyed many fine games together, both playing off the same single-figure handicap. We even began what we called 'a world series', meeting up at convenient midway points while we were both en route to different matches. In one game, at Moretown near Headingley, we had a ding-dong encounter that saw me three down with three to play. But I managed to raise my game at the crucial time and I parred the remaining holes, while Chris, much to his frustration, dropped a shot on each hole, allowing me to halve the match. I built up a lead of 6-4 in our challenge, but sadly my matches with Chris in 1999 were our final games together as he died the following winter.

I've also had some classic encounters at Finchley Golf Club in north London, where David Brown, the club's professional, kindly made arrangements for cricketers and umpires to play on the course. On one occasion I was playing against Merv Kitchen, and the fun began right on the very first hole – a short par four. I started by hitting a three iron straight down the middle, while 'Kitch' pushed his ball out into the right-hand rough. I had the right to play first, so I took out a wedge and was happy to see the ball fly towards the flag. Merv saw it going into the air, and then turned to address his ball. To my delight, I watched my ball drop into the hole, but Merv was oblivious to my fantastic start. He chipped his ball into the air, watched it land on the green and roll slowly towards the hole. Feeling quite satisfied with his shot, Merv then started to look around to see where my ball had landed. After several desperate glances, Merv turned round to me and asked, 'Where's your ball B.J.? Have you gone through the back?' Keeping a straight face, I replied, 'No Kitch. It's in the hole!' 'Never,' said an incredulous Merv, as he headed off towards the green, still thinking that I was pulling his leg. But then he was simply lost for words as he walked over to the hole to see my ball nestling there!

By this time, however, I had discovered pastures new, and had found plenty of chances to develop my golfing skills on the beautiful courses in South Africa. This was because from the 1980s I had returned on a regular basis to the republic to assist in their umpire development programme. It had all begun in August 1982, shortly after I had returned home after standing in the Test match between England and Pakistan at Headingley. I was naturally quite tired and my head was still full of what had gone on over the course of the five-day match. However, I soon had something else to think about as Gillian said that Dr Ali Bacher had been trying to get hold of me so that he could discuss an invitation to go out to South Africa during the winter months to assist in their umpire development programme. It subsequently transpired that Dr Bacher had negotiated with the South African Cricket Umpires' Association for an English umpire to visit the Cape for four months between December and March to have some input, especially into umpire-player relationships. Lord's had recommended both Kenny Palmer and myself as being well equipped to do the job. But Kenny apparently wasn't too keen to do the lecturing side of the visit and, shortly after getting the full details from Dr Bacher, I accepted the job.

At the time, South Africa were still banned from playing Test cricket because of apartheid, and there was plenty of coverage in the Press in the UK about the English cricketers who went out to the Cape in the winter months to either play or coach. Several tours had also been organised, with the ruling authorities banning the players concerned from Test cricket because of their contact with South Africa and involvement in these so-called 'rebel' tours. A few journalists in the UK started to make noises about banning everyone who had any links with the Cape and, after I had spent some time in the republic, there were also a few stories about me being banned from standing as an umpire in Test cricket.

But I wasn't a player or a coach – my case was completely different from that of the players, because I was acting solely as an individual, engaged in beneficial work with other officials and umpires. There were few controls on trade links at the time with South Africa and, as I was selling sport not politics, I was acting in the same way as countless thousands of other British men with business links in South Africa.

I'm glad to say that all the time I was working in South Africa, the TCCB kept in touch with me, and no issue was ever raised as far as my position was concerned. I don't know where these rumour-mongers got their information from, but I was never involved in any talks or threats about being blacklisted or taken off the Test panel because of my links with South Africa. I continued with my duties as an individual each winter out in the republic, and the powers-that-be accepted it and allowed me to continue my visits there each British winter. Despite all of this adverse publicity from the Press back home, spending the winter months in South Africa was never a decision I came to regret.

Umpiring in South Africa

My role during the winter months of 1982/83 initially involved travelling to various parts of South Africa, visiting schools and clubs to talk about umpiring, as well as standing in various league matches. It proved to be a very enjoyable time, especially as I had the chance to visit many old friends, as well as players from the county circuit who, like me, were wintering in the Cape.

In fact, the first two people I met after arriving in Cape Town were two English Test cricketers – Graham Gooch and John Emburey. I had bumped into them at Newlands as I was heading for the offices of the Western Province Cricket Association. They were both very pleased to see me, and immediately told me that they hadn't been too impressed with what they had seen so far with the umpiring in South Africa.

During my umpiring tour in the Cape I was also asked to stand in some club and school games, including the prestigious Nuffield Week, when the cream of talent from the schools in all of the provinces annually came together for various matches from which a South African Schools XI was chosen each year to play the host province, which that year was Boland. I had never umpired any schools' cricket before, but it was a real pleasure to see some very talented young boys, including Mark Rushmere, Daryl Cullinan and Andrew Hudson, and also to watch these youngsters play against the Boland side, which included Eddie Barlow and Kim Barnett of Derbyshire, who was spending the off-season with the province. It proved to be a wonderful game of cricket, and a most enjoyable experience.

The Nuffield Week was held that year in Stellenbosch, a beautiful university town in one of the most picturesque parts of South Africa, and it was a real pleasure to stand in these games at Oude Libertas and Groot Drakenstein – superb grounds with stunning views. I had visited the Drakenstein ground before when coaching out in the Cape in 1965. Going back there reminded me of a funny incident when I was involved in a game at the ground on the rest day of the South Africa *v.* England Test. The game was a friendly between a Press XI and an invitation side. I was asked to keep for the Press XI, who included both Denis Compton, who was covering the tour for a national newspaper, and Martin Young, my old Gloucestershire teammate, who was just starting his journalistic and broadcasting career in the Cape. 'Compo' was in a very relaxed mood, and had a spell bowling a series of quite slow deliveries to a left-hander. But as the balls got slower the length got shorter and, to one of these long hops, the left-hander to my horror swung completely around and smashed the ball towards me. It hit me a glancing blow on the head and cannoned off to the boundary for four. I staggered around, much to my colleagues' amusement, before falling down rather dazed. I soon recovered though, and was able to see straight again, but Martin and several others were still doubled up in mirth!

After this initial visit, I regularly returned to South Africa, largely because of one man – Denzil Bezuidenhout, the president of the Natal Cricket Umpires' Association. During my initial visit, I spent three weeks in Durban based at the Royal Hotel, and quickly got involved in umpiring in Natal. I was met at the airport by Ken Sutler-Gore, a member of the Durban and Districts Cricket Umpires' Association, who immediately hauled me off to umpire a Kingsmead Mynah game.

It was Ken who also introduced me to Denzil, who I had seen the previous day on television standing in a game in Cape Town, and with whom I had dinner early in my stay in Durban. Denzil was a complete stranger to me, but we had instant rapport. He soon put me at ease and not only did he make me feel comfortable, but he made me feel important. He even shared my taste in music! It was a very pleasant three weeks in Durban, as I stood with the local umpires and went through the same programme of talks as I had undertaken in other parts of the republic. Everyone was so welcoming, especially Denzil and, towards the end of my stay, he asked me if I would consider returning in October 1983 to work for the Natal Cricket Umpires' Association.

Before departing for the UK, I told Denzil that I would be happy to accept his offer, provided the terms of his contract were similar to those offered by Dr Bacher. They were, and that was the start of my regular visits to South Africa and the forming of a firm friendship with Denzil – both of which were factors in my decision on retiring as a first-class umpire in England to emigrate to Kwa-Zulu Natal. I had five happy 'seasons' working for the Natal Umpires' Association until 1987/88, when Dr Bacher contacted Denzil asking if I could be relieved from my duties in Durban to become Director of Umpiring for South Africa. Denzil readily agreed and I was honoured to accept the post of national director and co-ordinator of the South African Cricket Umpires' Association.

The Press gave a fair amount of coverage to my new appointment, and it was quite humbling to read the nice things people were saying. One example was a report in the *Natal Mercury*, which claimed that I had been enlisted 'to help rid the men in the middle of the stigma attached to the last season, when they were called amateurs adjudicating a professional game. According to SACUA's Ted Wood, "last season our umpiring was in tatters. We were told to put our house in order and we have enlisted the aid of the very best in Barrie Meyer."'

My new role involved standing in Currie Cup fixtures, as well as continuing to give lectures and seminars to umpires' organisations, schools and universities throughout the country. The previous year, no less than thirty-nine different people had stood in first-class matches. Now a fourteen-man panel had been formed, with eight people standing in the Currie Cup matches and six others in the Bowl fixtures. It was a far more streamlined system, but there were still several other issues to overcome, especially trying to establish mutual respect between the players and the umpires.

In my very first Currie Cup match, I had first-hand experience of some of the difficulties faced by the local umpires. The game in question was Western Province *v.* Transvaal at Newlands, on 31 December – the visitors were led by Clive Rice, who played for Nottinghamshire, and they also included Warwickshire's Alvin Kallicharran and Worcestershire's Neal Radford. For their part Western Province had two England men – Graham Gooch and John Emburey – as well as Derbyshire's Peter Kirsten, Kent's Roy Pienaar and Stephen Jefferies, who played for Hampshire and Lancashire. But, after one of the morning sessions, there was an unfortunate incident involving Barry Smith, my fellow umpire, who had travelled down from Natal. Alvin Kallicharran, who had bowled the final over before lunch from Barry's end, had snatched his hat from Barry and, as we left the field for lunch, I noticed that a few words had been exchanged. Barry was not his usual self over lunch, and he told me that he did not want to umpire after lunch, and wasn't prepared to take any more abuse from 'Kalli' regarding his

umpiring ability. I told Barry that I would see if I could sort out this problem, and duly went to the door of the Transvaal dressing room and asked for
their coach Ronnie Eriksen, who I then told to come down to our dressing room with 'Kalli' because I wanted to speak to both of them. However,
only Eriksen initially came down, who said that he wanted to apologise on
Kallicharran's behalf. But I wasn't too happy with this, and asked Eriksen to
go back and bring 'Kalli' down in person. Alvin duly arrived, said that he
had been out of order and apologised to me. I replied, 'Alvin, you should
be apologising to Mr Smith, not to me.' He did so, and that was the end of
the matter, but I later told Barry that he should deal immediately with a
cricketer if they stepped out of line, making it firmly clear that he would
not take any more abuse.

There was another incident during this game that alerted me to other
umpiring issues. It happened after Graeme Pollock had arrived at the wicket
with Transvaal 37 for 2. Soon after Pollock had played himself in, Garth Le
Roux, who I knew from his time with Sussex, bowled a magnificent delivery
to Pollock that pitched round about off-stump and swung in a little bit before
hitting Pollock on the move, around middle and off. Pollock was absolutely
plumb lbw – one of the easiest decisions I ever had to give but, as I raised my
finger, Le Roux stopped his appeal and swung around and said to me 'I can't
believe that.' Initially, I thought Le Roux was questioning my decision, but
he then told me afterwards that he had had Pollock out leg-before so many
times in the past, but it seemed that the umpires were reluctant to uphold
the appeal against such an iconic figure in South African cricket. Evidence
clearly that the local umpires were overawed by many players.

As I saw several times during my stay in the Cape, some umpires did not
have the respect of the players. Indeed, after this match between Western
Province and Transvaal, Vintcent van der Bijl, the great Springbok bowler,
came up to me and invited me to join his victorious Transvaal team in their
dressing room. It transpired that they had been highly impressed with the fact
that I had called them all by name as they came to the wicket and during the
time they were fielding. This was something that was obviously new to them,
but it was, after all, the accepted and common practice in the UK. In fact, I
always found it much easier to deal with players by being on first-name terms
or using their nickname. They accept you more readily and, in any case, it is far
more polite than coldly addressing them as 'batsman' or 'bowler'.

There were other occasions when the local umpires did not deal with
certain situations in a strong enough manner. A case in point was the Currie

Cup final at The Wanderers between Transvaal and Western Province – a match that Transvaal only had to draw in order to regain the cup. Western Province batted first and declared on 280 for 7 before Transvaal gained a first-innings lead by making 340 for 7 and Western Province went in again. They were desperate for quick runs as it was their only hope of forcing a win and securing the cup. But it was at this point that Alan Kourie, the Transvaal quick bowler, decided that he was going to waste a bit of time by continuing his follow-through until he was almost up to the batsman before he walked back to his bowling mark. I was standing at square-leg and, initially, was unable to do anything, but eventually I caught the eye of local umpire Karl Liebenberg, and asked him to meet me halfway for a chat. We conferred and both agreed that Kourie was time-wasting, and called over Clive Rice, the Transvaal captain, to sort the matter out with him. But Clive's attitude was that there was not a problem as Kourie's over rate was up to standard. I replied that according to law 42 and the Spirit of Cricket, Kourie was time-wasting, and that was what I was concerned with, not his over rate. I then asked Clive to do something about it, otherwise I would. He gave a little smile of acknowledgement, and he did sort the matter out because, from then on, Kourie did not have such an exaggerated follow-through.

At the end of the day, Western Province made enough to set Transvaal a target of 214 in four hours, but their bowlers could not make any inroads and, with the Transvaal top order content to play for a draw, they were 176 for 2 with 10 overs to go when the light deteriorated and Karl and I called time, leaving Transvaal to celebrate their fourth Currie Cup in five seasons. Had I not intervened as strongly as I did, the game could have ended with ill-feeling between the teams, and it showed to Karl, who deservedly went on to become one of the ICC's Test panel, the benefits of nipping something in the bud and acting firmly. It was also an example of something that I feel very strongly about, namely that the art of umpiring is, in my mind, to control the game without being officious.

'I SELL SPORT, NOT POLITICS'

Another aspect of my duties as national director and co-ordinator of the South African Cricket Umpires' Association was to act as an observer at the major domestic matches, and it was wearing this 'hat' that I watched the B&H night series first semi-final tie between Natal and Transvaal at

Kingsmead in March 1991. It was a good contest, and ended up with Natal's Jonty Rhodes requiring 7 runs to win off the last ball, bowled by Richard Snell. The bowler thought that all he had to do was to bowl a yorker but, coming in off a short run, he let the ball go a little bit too early and it turned out to be a full toss instead. It came through to Rhodes above waist height and, quickly picking up the flight of the ball, he swivelled around and hit the ball over the mid-wicket boundary for six.

Most of the spectators, and the Transvaal fielders, thought that they had won because, with the scores level, they had lost fewer wickets, which under the regulations was the tie-break if the scores were level. As the ball disappeared into the crowd, some of the Transvaal fans ran onto the outfield to celebrate with their team, but Jonty Rhodes remained at the crease with a broad smile on his face. I then noticed that Hennie de Bruin, the square-leg umpire, had his arm outstretched signalling a no-ball, with Rudi Koertzen, at the bowler's end, nodding in Hennie's direction to confirm the height of the ball and the decision to call it as an illegal delivery. I was impressed with their decision-making, as it had been a brave call and they could quite easily have let the situation go or, as in the past, backed down under pressure.

Some of the Transvaal players had even started to sprint off to the pavilion to start celebrating their success, but their joy was short-lived, as they had to troop back to the middle for the final delivery. There was a small delay, however, as a new ball and a replacement set of stumps were found – the originals had disappeared among the premature celebrations. While waiting for the new ones to appear, a few words were exchanged between Jimmy Cook, the Transvaal captain, and the umpires. From my vantage point I could clearly see that Jimmy was fuming, and I later discovered he was angry about what he perceived to be a late call, after the ball had gone for six. But both Hennie and Rudi were absolutely correct with their interpretation, as the playing regulations stated 'either umpire shall call and signal no ball if any full toss passes or would have passed the striker's wicket above stump height.'

Rhodes duly took guard again, and Snell had to run in again to deliver the last legal ball. Transvaal needed it to be a dot ball, so Snell tried another yorker in an attempt to win the game but, yet again, it turned out to be a full toss, though not as high as his previous delivery. As before, Rhodes picked up the ball as quick as a flash and flicked it over mid-wicket to give Natal a remarkable victory and send them through. But that was not the end of the matter, as controversy reigned as the players and officials returned to the pavilion with Alan Kourie, the irate Transvaal coach, directing some angry words in the direction of the umpires. I witnessed his outburst as I had decided to pop into the umpires' room to compliment them on the way they had handled themselves and for following the playing conditions and laws in order to make the right decisions.

After I had said my words of congratulations, Kourie burst in and was quite rude to the officials, complaining that they had not called one or two similar full tosses when Transvaal were batting. He had no right to be there, never mind say what he did, and I told him so, adding further that if he wanted to argue with anyone, it should have been with his bowler for twice bowling full tosses. Kourie was subsequently hauled before an impromptu disciplinary committee because of these angry remarks, but all ended well, with the two teams sharing a few beers together afterwards, giving Rhodes a chance to console Snell.

The introduction of this playing condition for one-day games with a full toss being called a 'no ball' was based on its good use in limited-overs competitions in English cricket. It also stemmed from developments in the way that county players tried to stop runs being scored. When the Sunday League began in 1969, many of the county cricketers were still learning about the correct tactics in these limited-overs games. In the early matches in the Gillette Cup, introduced in 1963, some players adopted similar tactics to those employed in the ordinary three-day game and, even when the Sunday League began, such an approach was still used by some teams, with a game between Somerset and Essex at Taunton seeing Brian Langford, the West Country spinner, returning bowling figures of 8-8-0-0. It therefore took time for the players to realise that the limited-overs form of the game is more defensive than the longer form, and captains needed to employ defensive fields rather than always trying to get the batsmen out. As a more defensive approach came in, some bowlers began bowling deliberately down the leg side in an attempt to prevent batsmen from hitting the ball, and then others began bowling bouncers as this is a type of ball that is almost impossible to hit and therefore score runs from. Initially, there were no regulations in the playing conditions that umpires could refer to in order to penalise this negative approach, but over time, in consultation with the umpires' panel, the TCCB introduced some sensible policies that stopped bowlers delivering full tosses, bouncers or leg-side deliveries in one-day games. Bowlers may feel that many of the modern regulations are stacked in favour of the batsmen but, by reducing the number of full tosses and bouncers, it has put an onus on what I consider real bowling skills, and I feel the game is far better for the introduction of these playing conditions.

The 1990/91 season had been a hectic one. Besides acting in an advisory capacity to the South African umpires, I also oversaw training courses and travelled around talking to clubs and other groups, all with the goal of trying to ensure that umpires, at whatever level, engaged in good practice, and gained the respect and trust of the participants. The 1990/91 season was also an historic one as, in July 1991, the ICC admitted South Africa back into the 'family' of Test cricket, and it therefore went down in the history books as the last summer of isolation. Following the abolition of apartheid, I had seen many changes, especially people's attitude to each other, which resulted in the satisfactory situation now being upheld in the republic. But I was not a politician and, as a sportsman – albeit in the guise of an official rather than a participant – I was there to ensure fair play in the country's sporting arenas. As other changes took place in the political and social arenas, I was delighted to see the way umpiring standards rose and the way the programmes that I had devised began to bear fruit. My efforts seemed to be paying off and, as in my umpiring career, I was getting it right! However, not everyone was happy with what I had done in South Africa during the 1980s, and it still rather irked me to read articles that suggested that I should be penalised for my links with the republic. One even claimed that 'The TCCB confirmed a report that Barrie Meyer, who had stood in 18 Tests and is at present national director and co-ordinator of the South African Cricket Umpires' Association, has been told to cut his links or face a six-year ban.'

It was while I was in South Africa that I had also seen Test cricket move into the technological age as, during the first Test of the 1992/93 season, between South Africa and India, Sachin Tendulkar, the great Indian batsman, had been adjudged run out by Jonty Rhodes after the use of television replays. At the time, Sachin was on 11, with his team struggling on 38 for 2. He had played the ball just backward of square and had set off for a run, but Jonty had bounded in swiftly to pick up the ball. Seeing Jonty gather, Sachin changed his mind and, as Jonty sent a hard flat throw back towards the stumps, Sachin tried to regain his ground. In the meantime Andrew Hudson, who had been fielding at short-leg, had moved swiftly up to the stumps, and he took the return throw from Jonty on the bounce and broke the wicket. Sachin had his bat outstretched and, from my position in the stands, it was a desperately close decision. I was pleased that Cyril Mitchley at square-leg immediately made up his mind to refer the decision to third umpire, Karl Liebenburg, who was watching the television monitor in the umpires' room. After twenty seconds or so, the replays made it crystal clear that Sachin had not regained his ground, and Karl pressed the button for a green light – at that time, the authorities had decided upon following the traffic light principle of a green light for go, and a red light for staying put.

As it turned out, the margin of this particular decision was less than a foot and, in the flurry of activity, I doubt if any umpire in the world would have been able to say with 100 per cent certainty whether Sachin was in or out. Without the television replays, I for one would have probably given Sachin the benefit of the doubt, and would have said 'not out'. But the television replays now provided clear proof that Sachin was in fact short of his ground, and I was pleased that there was a minimum of delay in reaching the correct decision, especially as it swiftly removed any lingering element of doubt, as well as any potential controversy.

The match also saw another ICC experiment with the home umpires being rotated to allow them to have a break from on-field action. Steve Bucknor of the West Indies stood on all five days, but Cyril Mitchley and Karl Liebenburg took it in turns to stand with him. This innovation was, I felt, far less successful than using technology to assist with line decisions. Despite being very good and experienced officials, both Cyril and Karl lost continuity and did not feel that they were taking a full part in the match. There was also evidence of inconsistency in decision-making, which was not good for the game, and I was very pleased when the ICC decided to halt this experiment.

Other commentators on the game have subsequently called for another trial in rotating umpires, but I'm still firmly of the belief that, if an umpire cannot stand for five days in a Test match environment, he should not be there in the first place. The creation of an ICC world panel of umpires to stand in Test matches has helped enormously and now the best men are standing throughout the year, adjudicating on the actions of the world's best players. With technology being fully embraced worldwide, it has also meant that there have been fewer and fewer controversial decisions.

As far as the English panel of county umpires is concerned, the creation of an ICC elite group has meant that some of England's officials have not stood in as many domestic games as in previous years. I knew from my time in both England and later in South Africa that the less experienced junior umpires learnt a great deal out in the middle by standing with another umpire who was the veteran of many Test matches or one-day internationals. Luckily, we have so many senior umpires in England that there has always been a vast pool of experience for our younger colleagues to draw upon. Because we play so much, compared with other countries, the more inexperienced umpires can also quite quickly witness the subtly different methods of dealing with each situation that a more senior colleague may have, and this has allowed the younger officials to relatively quickly sort out which approach works best for them. The introduction of technology in televised games has also helped them, and I'm delighted to have played my part in helping to ensure that the men in white coats, in both England and South Africa, were generally getting it right.

NINE

My World Squad

The Batsmen and Wicketkeepers

We can all sit down and pick our all-time world XI. Similar names are likely to appear, but it's always difficult to compare players from different eras. The game has changed so much that it is difficult to make a decision between someone from the early 1900s with a great player from the past decade or two. With this in mind, I've decided to choose a squad of twenty-four players based solely on my time while playing and officiating in county and international matches, and I'll let you choose two teams, complete with a twelfth man game, for an imaginary Super Test or, if you prefer, a one-day.

I make no apologies by starting with the two wicketkeepers. I guess it was natural for me, as a former member of the wicketkeepers' union, to pay a great deal of attention to the standard of glove work while I was standing in county games and Test matches. When I began umpiring, England were blessed with two keepers of the highest class – Alan Knott of Kent and Bob Taylor of Derbyshire. When playing, I had seen John Murray put in some wonderful performances for Middlesex, while Jim Parks was a fine 'keeper for Sussex, but Alan and Bob were truly outstanding, with each displaying sheer natural ability.

When I was umpiring matches involving Kent, I found it fascinating to watch Alan keep wicket to Derek Underwood and, even when standing up on a spiteful, turning wicket, Alan always gave a faultless display. Bob too was an immaculate keeper, always neat and tidy whether up or back to the stumps. I was fortunate to witness at first hand one of his finest performances, keeping for England in the Headingley Test of 1981 and, like Alan, Bob was a super guy off the field – very friendly, very sociable and a credit to the game.

It was fascinating as well for me to observe how the really top-class batsmen got their runs. Because each was a different character, they all had
different ideas on how they wanted to play the game. Take Graham Gooch
and Geoffrey Boycott for example – both were fine opening batsmen, but
they had vastly different methods. Boycott simply wanted to stay at the
crease for as long as possible. If you bowled 6 good length balls to him,
he would play them back quietly with respect, but if you bowled him a
half-volley or long hop, he would pounce on these loose balls and hit them
for boundaries. Graham Gooch was very different and, in May 1994, I witnessed an exceptional innings by the Essex run-machine in their four-day
match at Chelmsford against Kent. On a wicket that helped the spin bowlers, Goochie scored 236 – the tenth double-century of his career – which
helped to lay the foundation of a sizeable total. Together with Paul Prichard,
Gooch added 316 for the first wicket and completely dominated the two
Kent spinners, Carl Hooper and Min Patel.

But Gooch's contribution was not restricted to the first innings as, in their
second innings, Essex needed 50 to win and, with the wicket almost turning
square, Hooper and Patel took 3 wickets each. But Gooch was the master
once again and, despite the clatter of wickets around him, he smashed 37
out of the 50 runs needed to guide his side to a remarkable victory. While
standing in Test matches, I saw Graham score a fine 154 against the 1990
New Zealanders at Edgbaston, as well as an excellent 120 against the 1993
Australians at Trent Bridge. I also saw him compile a couple of very good
centuries against Australia in one-day internationals at Lord's – an unbeaten
117 in 1985, followed by 136 in 1989. But it was another hundred at Lord's,
in the Test against the 1980 West Indians, that I consider to have been the
best that I witnessed at first-hand by Graham. On this particular occasion, I
was standing with Bill Alley, the former Somerset batsman who, in his day,
had been a fine and courageous batsman himself against the quicks. As we
prepared ourselves in the umpires' room before the start of the match, Bill
and I reminisced about the fast bowlers of our time, with Bill recounting
some of his encounters as a youngster in Australia. But, even in his time,
Bill did not have to cope with four fast and extremely hostile bowlers, as
the West Indians of 1980 boasted. Their attack for this Test comprised Andy
Roberts, Michael Holding, Joel Garner and Colin Croft – a ferocious and
awesome unit, and one that gave the batsmen no respite.

They were soon into their stride, with the graceful Michael Holding
having Geoff Boycott caught behind for 8. But Graham was equal to the

challenge – playing with calm authority, he was quick to judge the length, driving with great power off the front foot and hooking with great purpose anything short of a length. With Chris Tavare dropping anchor at the other end, Graham reached his century – his first at Test level – before being trapped leg-before by Holding for 123. A measure of his complete domination of this fearsome attack was that England's total stood at 165, and none of their other batsmen went on to pass fifty in this match. This match also featured another fine hundred by a batsman with a totally different method, as Viv Richards, on his first appearance in a Test at Lord's, made a dazzling 145. Viv was perhaps the greatest batsman I ever saw, yet he would block a half volley then hit a length ball for four – that's how he played. A big innings from Viv would contain some remarkable strokes, and I can still remember a quite unbelievable one he played at the same ground in the 1979 World Cup final. There was one ball to go in the West Indies' innings with Mike Hendrick bowling the final over from my end. As he walked past me back to his mark, 'Hendo' said to me, 'Where do you think I should bowl this one then B.J.?' I replied that I always believed a yorker around off stump to be a good ball to bowl because few batsmen were able to do much about that. 'Hendo' duly took heed of my advice and delivered a very full-length delivery right on off stump, but Viv nonchalantly pirouetted in his stance, and scooped the ball behind square for six. To this day, I still do not know how Viv actually managed to hit the ball – it was truly an unbelievable shot.

In the 1980 Test at Lord's against England, he played a similar range of quite audacious and breathtaking shots, including four boundaries in one over from the fine Kent spinner Derek Underwood, who had been recalled to the Test team by the selectors in a bid to restrict the Caribbean run machine. England's tactics against Viv were to restrict his scoring on the on-side, but their concentration on or around off stump merely gave Viv an opportunity to unfurl some exquisitely timed strokes on the off-side and, with the ball regularly disappearing through the covers, it was clear that England's plan had spectacularly backfired! In 1990 I witnessed another quite remarkable innings by Viv, this time in the county match between Hampshire and Glamorgan at Southampton, which had seen time being lost to the weather. But the two captains got their heads together and made a game of cricket never to be forgotten in my opinion. Mark Nicholas, the home captain, set Glamorgan a target of 363 and, with their score on 139 for 5, it seemed like Glamorgan had little chance of winning. But Viv was still at the crease and, with Nigel Cowley proving to be an able partner, the runs started to tick over.

Obviously Viv was the dominant partner but Nigel played his part, chipping his singles and running hard as 167 runs were accrued to take Glamorgan closer to their target. If the Welsh county were to win, I thought that Viv would need to take even more of the strike, but he didn't seem to be too concerned, and even hit singles off the first ball of an over to give Nigel the strike! At one stage, I even thought that Viv had settled for the draw, and was letting Nigel block it out for a draw. Slowly but surely the runs kept coming and, although the asking rate had reached double figures, Viv still believed that Glamorgan could win – even when faced by his West Indian colleague Malcolm Marshall, who roared in for the final over with Glamorgan needing 14 to win. I had fully expected Viv to just play for the draw, but I had miscalculated because he despatched Marshall for four, six and another four to astonishingly see Glamorgan home with a couple of balls to spare. As Viv walked off, the crowd, to a man, rose in appreciation of his innings, which had been a masterpiece of aggression, brutal timing, calculation and sheer genius. If ever I see a better innings than on that day at the now-defunct Northlands Road ground, I will be very surprised.

Another member of the Richards clan – Barry – was also an awesome batsman, capable of destroying the finest of county attacks. I mentioned earlier Barry's wonderful double-hundred for Hampshire against Lancashire at Southport in July 1973. The home side were dismissed for 214 before Barry and Gordon Greenidge shared a double-century opening stand. Three times during his innings, strokes from Barry's bat landed onto the roofs of neighbouring houses, with the tiles disintegrating under the bombardment they received from B.A. Richards. But Barry was not just a batsman who deposited balls out of the ground with powerful shots – he could also hit them, or should I say caress them, with immaculate timing to the boundary, with strokes that were straight out of the coaching manual. On this particular day at Southport, he struck 19 fours in a perfect example for any watching schoolboys of how to play the right shot at the right time in what became a slaughter of the Lancashire attack.

Another opening batsman in my world squad is Gordon Greenidge – his unbeaten 214 at Lord's in 1984 was masterly and, to be honest, I do not think I ever saw a Test attack so completely dominated by one man as on that day. Gordon had an immaculate technique and could play some scorching square cuts, as well as beautifully timed and quite delicate strokes in an arc between cover point and mid-wicket. His wonderful innings at Lord's saw the West Indians reach their target of 344 in five-and-a-half hours for the loss of just a single wicket and completely confound the predictions of the critics, who felt that the target was out of reach. In fact, before we took the field, David Evans and I had a chat in the umpires' room about what might happen, and we agreed that the most likely outcome to the contest was a draw, but we had clearly reckoned without Gordon's brilliance. Later in that series, Gordon showed another side of his game by batting for almost 10 hours to save the Test at Old Trafford. His second double century of the series was testament to his marvellous temperament and his many years of batting on English surfaces with Hampshire.

I would also choose Gordon's opening partner Desmond Haynes in my world squad. I was lucky enough to see him make a superb 184 in the Lord's Test in 1980, during which he shared a second-wicket partnership of 233 with Viv Richards. In all, Dessie batted for over 8 hours and his efforts helped to lay the foundations of a formidable total in excess of 500. Throughout his stoic innings, Dessie remained sharply focused but, while at the non-striker's end, he was always prepared for a bit of banter with me and, as always, a smile was never too far away from his face. This was one occasion where his opening partnership with Gordon yielded just 1 run. In 89 Tests, they averaged 47.32 and their success opening the batting was, in my view, equally as important a factor in the West Indians' success in Test cricket during the 1980s as their fearsome four-pronged pace attack.

No world squad would be complete without Graeme Pollock, who I first saw on my journeys to South Africa in the 1960s, and on the Springboks' tour to England in 1965. The tall, elegant left-hander would effortlessly despatch even the good balls for a boundary, and I still remember the talk on the county circuit after his remarkable 125 in the Test at Trent Bridge in 1965. The overcast conditions that day were tailor-made for the English seamers, especially Tom Cartwright, who quickly reduced the tourists to 43 for 4. But, in the following couple of hours, Graeme made a complete mockery of what had gone before him and, despite the conditions assisting the English attack, he proceeded to register a stunning century and tamed Cartwright's devilish seam and swing. Graeme was still playing in the early 1980s when I returned to South Africa, although the years in between had not seen him perform on the Test stage, and it is a matter of conjecture how many hundreds Graeme might have made in Test cricket. Despite being into his forties, he was still good enough to make a superb 108 in a one-day international at Johannesburg in 1985/86 against a 'rebel' Australian attack.

I'll choose another graceful left-hander – David Gower – as the next batsman in my world squad. David was one of the most elegant stroke-makers during my time as a Test and county umpire, and I had the privilege of seeing him record his maiden Test hundred in July 1979 at Edgbaston as David made a sublime 200* against an attack that boasted Kapil Dev, Srini Venkataraghavan and Bhagwat Chandrasekhar. None of these Indian masters bothered the blond-haired Englishman, whose silky strokeplay helped his side to amass a sizeable total from which they forced an innings victory, and all against an Indian batting line-up that contained the likes of Sunil Gavaskar, Dilip Vengsarkar and Gundappa Vishwanath. Despite the odd lapse outside off stump and, on rare occasions, lazy footwork, David was a prolific scorer at county level with Leicestershire and Hampshire, and he owed his success to an unflappable temperament and an ability to remain motionless at the crease before swiftly and easily moving into line and caressing the ball with the air of a magician. He also had an affable personality, so it was a delight to deal with David when he was acting as captain either at county or Test level.

I don't know what it is about left-handers, but I've chosen another one in Allan Border, the elegant and pugnacious Australian batsman, who also had spells in county cricket with Gloucestershire and Essex. His concentration and determination were legendary and, even in a relatively mundane county fixture, he would show the same intensity and purpose as when batting for Australia. A.B.'s prolific run-scoring saw Australia recover from the lean years of the early 1980s to a position a few years later where the only superior side in world cricket were the West Indies. I had first-hand experience of Allan's remorseless and tenacious accumulation of runs at The Oval in the 1981 series with England. In that particular Test, he came within 16 runs of scoring a century in each innings. After making an unbeaten 106 in the first innings, he continued his domination of the English attack of Bob Willis, Mike Hendrick, Ian Botham and John Emburey in the second innings before falling to the latter for 84. During that summer, he was comfortably the best batsman on either side, and he was often at his best in adversity, as at Manchester where he overcame the pain and discomfort of a broken finger to make a most courageous 123 not out. He may have been in a side that year that lost the Ashes, but he had the pleasure in 1982/83 of their return to Australia.

There are several most worthy candidates for the final batting berth in my world squad. I never saw Sachin Tendulkar while I was out on the field, but many times I have marvelled at the prolific Indian while watching matches either from the stands or on television. I was also highly impressed while standing in matches by the gifted Pakistani Javed Miandad, who could play some truly audacious strokes, and also Brian Lara of the West Indies – and it is the latter's sheer weight of runs, and appetite for the really long innings, that have won the day. I had the pleasure of seeing Brian on his first tour of England with the West Indians in 1991, and then again for Warwickshire on the county circuit. You only had to watch him bat for a few overs to realise that Brian had a masterful technique that, allied to his strong wrists and sure footwork, allowed him to unerringly place the ball, almost at will, on either side of the wicket. Even on his first visit to England, his trademark whip stroke off his hips was played with such panache and elegance that I noted the name of Brian Charles Lara down as someone who would be a real force in Test cricket. Subsequent events confirmed my judgement, and he remained an iconic figure in the 1990s at a time when West Indian cricket went on the decline – I'm sure only a temporary feature.

The Bowlers and Captains

Time now to pick the bowlers and captains in my world squad. On the bowling front, I'll start with the all-rounders for my teams, and I'll immediately choose Ian Botham and Sir Richard Hadlee. As I outlined earlier, I was lucky enough to see Ian's remarkable performances in the 1981 Ashes Series, and his stroke-play at Headingley was both awesome and awe-inspiring. I don't think that in my time as an international umpire I witnessed another innings that was so destructive in its intensity, nor one that so completely transformed the outcome of a match that seemed almost to be relentlessly heading towards the Australians. Two years before at the same venue, I witnessed Ian's latent talents as a Test batsman, as he made 137 in a shade over three-and-a-quarter hours against India. The match was badly affected by the weather, but Ian's savage assault on the Indian attack was rich entertainment, as he scored 99 in the pre-lunch session on the fourth day, pulling Kapil Dev over the pavilion and sweeping Bishan Bedi into the car park. His searing assault on the experienced Indian bowlers deservedly won Ian the Man of the Match award, and its adjudicator, Jim Laker, described his innings as 'one of the finest Test innings in the last twenty years'. Ian was also a highly talented swing bowler and, in the second Test I ever stood in

– the third match of the series with New Zealand in 1978 – Ian produced the magnificent figures of 6 for 101 and 5 for 39 as the visitors were beaten by 7 wickets. It was also the first time that we had been given light meters, but Dickie Bird and I did not have to use them as the match was played throughout in fine weather. Indeed, with little cloud cover, it was Ian's skills as a swing bowler that brought him his 11-wicket haul. Like everyone else I can only applaud Ian's dedication to charitable causes, especially those relating to leukaemia, and Ian's money-raising efforts in different parts of the world have been nothing short of awe-inspiring.

Richard Hadlee was a true gentleman, with a meticulous outlook on both batting and bowling. While with Nottinghamshire, he actually made a plan as to how he could achieve the double of 1,000 runs and 100 wickets in a season. His attention to detail was admirably rewarded as he reached his target in the last match of the season. From an umpiring point of view, he was very easy to work with as a bowler. He always knew exactly where his feet were landing and how close he was to overstepping. His line and length were immaculate – but that was typical of Sir Richard who, I believe, was one of the world's finest cricketers. He always gave 100 per cent, even in a losing cause, as with the fourth and final Test of the 1983 series with England – another match in which I stood with Dickie. New Zealand needed no less than 511 in their second innings and, when Richard arrived at the crease, they were already struggling on 184 for 6 and staring a record defeat in the face. Others might have hung around for a short while before hitting the ball in the air, but not Richard – despite having bowled 58 overs in England's two innings, he showed no sign of weariness and soon played some typically fierce straight drives. With only the lower order for company he almost doubled the total, with a defiant 92 not out off 118 balls. His efforts deserved a century, but he got his reward at the end of the match as he was named Cornhill's Man of the Series, having scored 477 runs at an average of 53, and taken 36 wickets at a shade under 24.

These were figures that Mike Procter, my former Gloucestershire colleague, could also have produced at international level had it not been for politics and South Africa's expulsion from the Test arena. A total of 226 Test runs and 41 wickets were scant reward for a man who was worth his place in the side either as a bowler or a batsman. And, in my view, he was the leading all-rounder in county cricket in the early 1970s. I can remember, right from his earliest days on the county's books, Mike had a great appetite for scoring hundreds. His straight drives and strokes through the covers were classically executed, and his finest innings in Gloucestershire's ranks came during the summer of 1971 when he hit four centuries. He began by recording a fine 133 against Leicestershire, and followed this up with a rapid century in just seventy-nine minutes against Middlesex. This proved to be the fastest hundred of the season, and his next century – against Somerset at Bristol – seemed almost pedestrian in comparison as he brought up three figures after a two-hour stay at the crease. His fourth century that summer – against Yorkshire at Sheffield – was undoubtedly the best, and it helped us achieve what had seemed at one stage an unlikely target of 201 in 135 minutes. When tea was taken, we had slumped to 28 for 3 and, with just eighty-five minutes' play remaining, a draw seemed the most likely result. But Mike was never one to shut up shop, and he returned to the crease after the interval and proceeded to smash 3 sixes and 17 fours in making a glorious hundred that saw us home with 2 overs to spare and 4 wickets in hand. Despite these wonderful efforts with the bat, Mike never shirked an opportunity with the new ball, and he was a tearaway bowler with a fast, whirlwind action that, like a catapult, would send the ball speeding out towards the batsman. As wicketkeeper, I soon got used to the slightly unconventional way he delivered the ball, almost chest-on and off the wrong foot. This flurry of arms and his unusual action appeared to surprise many county batsmen when they first faced him, but he beat many by his sheer pace as much as anything and, for the batsmen, it must have been quite an intimidating sight to see him charge towards the bowling crease with his blond mop of hair bobbing up and down. All 7 of Mike's Test caps were won in South Africa against Australia – on their visits in 1966/67 and again in 1969/70. I've often wondered what would have happened if Procter had locked horns at Test level with Gary Sobers, the great West Indian all-rounder who, like Mike, was a gifted batsman and a bowler who could deliver left-arm fast-medium, orthodox left-arm spin, or, just for extra variety, chinamen. During the 1960s and 1970s Gary played against Gloucestershire, and there were several occasions when these two great all-rounders played against each other. But to have watched these two wonderful cricketers head-to-head in Test cricket would have been fascinating.

Gary's first appearance against Gloucestershire at the County Ground came in 1963 on the West Indian tour, and I had the good fortune of catching him for just 3 off the lively bowling of David Smith. When the tourists bowled, Gary had a chance to display his bowling skills, and he took 4 wickets as Gloucestershire's experienced batting line-up – with the exception of

Martin Young, who made a fine century – struggled against the Caribbean attack. In 1968 he joined Nottinghamshire, and their visit to Bristol in June saw Gary up against Mike, who was batting at number four and opening the bowling. But the gods intervened and the three-day game was badly affected by rain. Gloucestershire made 175 for 4 with Mike making 26 and Gary ending up wicketless. The following year they met up again. The first time was when the West Indians visited Bristol in May but, once again, the weather had a say as rain washed out the first day's play. On the second day, Mike took 5 for 48 and bowled Gary with a beauty for a duck. But Gary got some revenge when later in the summer he returned to county action and visited Bristol with Nottinghamshire in July. It was his first innings of the summer for the country, and he gave an awesome display of batsman-ship, making a fine 98 and striking the ball with immense power. In all, he struck 17 fours, including 8 in his last 9 scoring strokes, and seemed destined to reach his century, but Mike returned to the attack and had Gary caught by David Smith when 2 runs short of the landmark. The inclement West Country weather then intervened again and there was no more play in the game, which was Tony Brown's Benefit match. It seemed that every time the two met up the weather intervened. But fortunately, both of our matches with Nottinghamshire in 1971 were unaffected by the weather, and I had the chance of seeing the two in action without any interruptions. It was worth waiting for as, in the first match at Newark, Mike top-scored in our first innings with a composed 58 before Gary erased the disappoint-ment of being run out for 6 on the first morning with a majestic 86, made on a wicket that was giving generous assistance to the spinners. But it was Mike who was the star of the return match at the Wagonworks ground in Gloucester, where he gave an exhilarating display of batting, making 115 and 70, while Gary, for once, ended up without a wicket and made just 14 and 7. Mike also had the final say, returning to the attack and claiming the final 2 wickets as Nottinghamshire were routed by 176 runs. Gary may not have shone on this final occasion where we played against each other, but I would have no hesitation in choosing him in my world squad – in fact I don't think I have seen such a complete cricketer as Gary.

I mentioned earlier the four-pronged West Indian pace attack that I saw against England in 1980. Despite their merits, both individually and col-lectively, I've chosen two other Caribbean pacemen in my world squad – Malcolm Marshall and Curtly Ambrose. Malcolm was, in my view, the greatest fast bowler that I ever saw play for the West Indies. His natural athleticism and whippy action allowed him to bowl with genuine pace and hostility that, allied to his knack of obtaining sharp swing and cut, made him a fearsome proposition. On several occasions in county matches, I saw 'Maco' use these abilities with Hampshire to work over a sequence of hard-ened batsmen, hustling the most experienced of openers with his sheer pace, before dissecting the middle-order with guile and cunning. The 1984 West Indian tour to England was his second Test series on these shores, and it was one in which he really came of age. I was standing at Lord's when his clever bowling with the old ball stifled England's ambitions after they had progressed to 101 without loss. But Malcolm made the early incision, removing Chris Broad and swiftly afterwards David Gower, before return-ing to the attack to add the scalps of Allan Lamb and Mike Gatting, as England's total slipped to 185, with all 4 wickets falling to M.D. Marshall. England never recovered after Maco's fine bowling, as they were dismissed for 286 with the pace bowler returning the fine figures of 35.5-10-85-6.

Curtly Ambrose was altogether a different proposition, but equally as effective. His sheer pace was derived from a classical high action, while his 6ft 7in frame allowed him to extract steepling bounce and skiddy pace on even the most benign of county wickets. When in full rhythm, Curtly could surprise the most experienced of batsmen with his sharp and nasty bouncer or fiendish yorker. Few batsmen on the county circuit ever played Curtly with complete authority and he always had the ability of wresting the psy-chological initiative away from the opposition. When standing in matches involving Northamptonshire when Curtly was their overseas player, I was often struck by the number of bowled and lbw decisions that went – quite correctly I should say – his way. The reason was quite simple: his priceless ability to surprise the opposition batting and to beat them with sheer pace.

During my playing career with Gloucestershire, England were blessed with many fine seam bowlers. But one man stood head and shoulders above them – the peerless Brian Statham, and the Lancashire seamer is my next choice in my world squad. Like all the great fast bowlers, Brian had a beau-tifully fluid and smooth action, allied to metronomic accuracy and an ability to make the ball move sharply both ways off the seam. I can still remember a county game against Lancashire during the late 1950s that took place on a slightly damp wicket at Bristol. After the great Lancashire bowler had taken several wickets, George Emmett told a group of young Gloucestershire professionals, including myself, to walk out with him to take a look at the wicket. As the wicket was a little bit moist, the ball had left a slight mark on the surface and, at the end to which Brian had been bowling, it was a real education to see a small cluster of tiny marks on the surface. They were so close together that George Emmett was able to reach into his pocket, get out a handkerchief, and then place it on the wicket, completely covering all of them. After getting to his feet, George didn't have to say anything to us impressionable youngsters and, in the subsequent years, I would have no hesitation in saying that Brian Statham was the finest English seam bowler that I faced during my playing career. In my time with Gloucestershire, we had many fine batsmen at the top of the order, but I know that none of them liked facing Brian. His career total – at a time when there were a host of outstanding county batsmen – of 2,260 first-class wickets at an average of 16.36, bore testament to his outstanding abilities and simple principle that, if the batsmen missed the ball, he would generally hit the stumps.

Late in my playing career, and then subsequently as an umpire, I became familiar with the superb fast-bowling talents of Dennis Lillee. Like the other pacemen in my world squad, Dennis had a fine action, culminating in a magnificent final leap in his delivery stride. He also had an outstanding physique and exceptional stamina, plus an extra ingredient – a dislike, bordering on hatred, of batsmen. There were times when his bristling aggression boiled over and he lost his rag, but he was equally as quick to smile again once he had regained his composure, and I never felt as an umpire that he harboured grudges for too long. Dennis was not just an out-and-out pace bowler, because he varied his pace and the direction of his swing with great guile and intelligence. He was a great showman as well, and there were times when he courted controversy, as in the Headingley Test of 1981 where he subsequently admitted that he and Rod Marsh had placed a bet, albeit at odds of 500/1, on Australia losing the match. But you would never have guessed this out in the middle, where from my position as umpire he was always the consummate competitor, full of fearsome deliveries, typically unleashed with a no-holds barred attitude, as well as the odd verbal quip to Ian Botham and his batting partners.

Later in my umpiring career in England, and also in South Africa, I was able to watch unfold the career of my other fast-bowling choice – Allan Donald. Even when his country were still in the international wilderness, I had seen enough in South African domestic cricket to agree with the verdict that Allan was the fastest white bowler in the world. Like Malcolm Marshall and Dennis Lillee, Allan was a natural athlete, with a beautiful action and great stamina. I was particularly impressed when officiating in games with

Allan how he liked to bowl long spells. Not for him a short burst and a lengthy graze in the outfield; instead, a long and probing spell, with each delivery asking the batsmen a searching question. Allan's other virtues were a tendency to bowl a fuller length than other international pacemen, as well as an ability to swing the ball sharply away from the bat, and I feel that these skills and his lion-hearted attitude would complement those of the other fast bowlers in my world squad.

On the spinning front, I would have no hesitation in naming Derek Underwood, of Kent and England, and Shane Warne, of Australia and Hampshire, in my squad. I never toured abroad and saw some of the great Indian or Pakistani spinners on their home surfaces but, from what I saw over the years in English conditions, I do not think that either Derek or Shane would let you down with the ball.

Derek Underwood, or 'Deadly' as he was known to several generations of county players, was not a classical slow bowler as his left-arm deliveries were made at a speed often closer to medium-pace. But his bowling had subtle variations of spin and trajectory and, on several occasions while batting for Gloucestershire, I was beaten by his clever arm ball that swung sharply into right-handers, and undid many better batsmen than me. There was something of a fast bowler in his make-up as 'Deadly' hated being scored off, and he often rattled off a sequence of maiden overs. These were skills that became highly valued in the limited-overs matches. In my first ever international match – the Prudential Trophy contest between England and Australia at Old Trafford in June 1977 – he produced a masterly spell of 11-1-29-3. His deft variations and nagging accuracy put a brake on the Australian batting, and none of their illustrious stroke-makers were at ease against him. The game also saw 'Deadly' briefly display his doggedness as a tail-ender, as England limped towards their target. Coming in at number ten, he stoutly defended and helped his Kent colleague, Alan Knott, steer England home to a narrow 2-wicket victory. It made something of a change for the two Kent men to combine forces with the bat. It was usually Knott the wicketkeeper who joined forces with Underwood the bowler and, as a member of the wicketkeepers' union, and later as an umpire, I was always impressed by Knotty's glove work to Deadly's spin bowling, and the way he cleverly and deftly read all of his variations – at times, I wondered if the two had a telepathic relationship!

I'm sure that Alan would have relished the opportunity to keep to my other spin choice – Shane Warne. Shane was just establishing himself in the Australian

side in my last couple of Tests. I stood in two of the Tests on their 1993 tour
– his first visit to England – and in my final Test, at The Oval, I saw Shane bowl
40 overs, albeit in a losing cause, as England won by 161 runs after sterling
bowling performances by two of the best England seam bowlers of the 1990s –
Gus Fraser of Middlesex and Glamorgan's Steve Watkin. Although there were,
at the time, a few rough edges to this particular bowling diamond, Shane's
outstanding skill as a wrist spinner was soon apparent, and I was fascinated to
see him go through his repertoire of stock leg-breaks, the flipper, the top-spin-
ner and googly. In my time as a county cricketer, most of the Championship
teams possessed a leg-spinner, but none were as fiercely competitive or as wily
as Shane, whose knack of making the ball grip and turn sharply away from the
right-handers, even on the most unresponsive surface, has few parallels.

Other contemporaries may offer alternative spin bowlers, including the
likes of Bishan Bedi, Chandrasekhar or Muralitharan, but I'm perfectly
happy with Shane as my front-line spinner. His outstanding powers of
spin, plus his ability to out-think batsmen, have been rewarded with a most
deserved record haul of wickets at Test level.

Finally, I need to choose two captains for my world teams. A captain must
be someone who is a fine player, a leader with a positive outlook, a good man-
manager, a person with a good sense of humour, self-confidence and a person
who is not afraid to lead by example. Although they may have the best vantage point on the field, I personally believed that wicketkeepers never made
the best captains. From my own experience, I felt that all my concentration and workload would have been directed to my specialist duties behind
the stumps, and I do not think that I would have maintained such a high
standard with the gloves on had I also to undertake the duties of captaincy.
I think, therefore, that it is no coincidence that most of the recent Test captains have been batsmen, and are people who can stand anywhere in the
field and focus totally on captaincy without having to bowl or keep wicket
themselves. I also have the same reservations over fast bowlers as captains.
Bob Willis of England led his country between 1982 and 1983, but I just
don't feel that fast bowlers can give 100 per cent attention on the field when
they are bowling flat out – in Bob's case, he could have bowled an over and
had a catch dropped, before calling for his sweater and walking away to his
fielding position. In his frustration at having not had a good over, I'm sure
he would have preferred to walk away focussing entirely on his own efforts
and individual role with the team, rather than having to walk away thinking
about organising the field from the other end.

Nevertheless, I am prepared to make an exception in the case of Imran Khan, who was more of an all-rounder than just a fast bowler, and was worth his place in the Pakistan side as either a batsman or as a bowler. He was a god-like figure in Pakistani cricket. Imran was a proud and dignified leader, who united a team with many different factions, as well as some volatile temperaments. He had a fine cricket brain, and was a keen competitor, always leading by example, striving to get the best out of the players in his charge. I first came across him towards the end of the my playing career, when he was initially playing county cricket with Worcestershire, before playing for Oxford University, and later switching to Sussex. Once he had got his eye in, Imran could be a destructive batsman and, on several occasions, I saw him effortlessly reel off a series of imperious strokes that transformed the course of a game, and lifted his side. He was also a match-winning bowler, bowling genuinely quick off a long run, with a high-leaping action. There were several times when I was standing in county games when Imran maintained this genuine pace over quite long spells. Some international pace bowlers would be happy to bowl flat out only for a short spell in county games, but not Imran – he would bowl genuinely quick for many overs. His sheer pace and ability to swing the ball meant that experienced county batsmen found him a handful. The same happened in Test matches, with Imran bowling long and hostile spells yet, despite all of these exertions, he still had firm control over his team, and was acutely aware of the demands of his side.

As far as the other captain of my world team is concerned, the choice would have to come from a shortlist including England's Mike Brearley, Ray Illingworth or Keith Fletcher, Steve Waugh of Australia, Clive Lloyd of the West Indies, and two South Africans – the late Hansie Cronje and Clive Rice. All were fine readers of the game, and none would let themselves down with the bat at Test level. But at the end of the day, the nod might just go to Clive Lloyd, who has gone down in history as one of the most successful captains of all time.

I saw Clive guide his wonderful team to the 1979 World Cup final at Lord's, and I stood in three of the matches when the West Indies had a 5-0 clean sweep over England in 1984. The talent at his disposal was outstanding, but there have been many other XIs with a lot of talent who have simply not gelled under a particular captain. In Clive's case, he unified a team bursting with strong personalities and powerful individuals and, on the field, he oversaw operations in a calm and dignified manner, always getting the best out of the rich talent at his disposal. There was also a paternal element to his approach, and he was very protective of his team. Yet when his pace attack had made the early incision, Clive would ensure that his team went for the jugular. Rarely under his firm leadership did the West Indies have the initiative wrested away from them once they had got on top and, as the outcome of the 1984 series in England showed, I witnessed some quite overwhelming victories by Clive's team. He was also a fine batsman, and often led from the front with a glittering display of quite brutal strokes, made with a heavy bat that at times resembled a railway sleeper. I had the pleasure of seeing his explosive range of shots on several occasions for the West Indians or Lancashire when playing against him, and later when standing in county and international matches. Clive also had something of a gangling figure and loping walk, yet he was an outstanding fielder who could pounce on a ball like a cat on a poor mouse before unleashing a powerful throw, which more often than not would directly hit the stumps. Woe betide any batsman who tried to pinch a quick single when 'Hubert' was patrolling the covers, and there were several occasions when I had the simplest of run-out decisions to make, as the batsmen were made to look foolish after an electrifying piece of fielding from Clive. This dynamic fielding, allied to his brilliant stroke-play and ruthless captaincy, makes him a most worthy member of my world squad.

So there we are; twenty-four great names who I saw during my time standing in Test, provincial and county matches, or while playing for Gloucestershire. I would have loved to have gone out to Australia, India or Pakistan either to play or umpire, as it would have given me a chance to watch some of the great names in action in their home conditions. But I never got the chance, so I have restricted my choice to people who I have seen – either in the UK or out in South Africa. Even so, their involvement in an imaginary game at Lord's – where else for a game of this magnitude? – and all at the peak of their form, would still make a most mouth-watering prospect.

I have deliberately not narrowed my choice down to just an XI, because the twenty-four names I have named in the past couple of chapters offer innumerable combinations of starting teams. To set the ball rolling, how about a one-day match between the two squads below, with Dickie Bird and David Shepherd as the two match umpires? I'd be very happy to be the third umpire, sitting in the umpires' room and looking at the television screens. I'll leave you to decide who should be the twelfth man in each squad, and whether the same two groups could then fight out a Test match. Happy choosing!

Squad A

C.G. Greenidge (West Indies)
D.L. Haynes (West Indies)
D.I. Gower (England)
B.C. Lara (West Indies)
R.G. Pollock (South Africa)
G. St.A. Sobers (West Indies)
Imran Khan (Pakistan – captain)
A.P.E. Knott (England – wicketkeeper)
R.J. Hadlee (New Zealand)
M.D. Marshall (West Indies)
S.K. Warne (Australia)
D.K. Lillee (Australia)

Squad B

G.A. Gooch (England)
B.A. Richards (South Africa)
A.R. Border (Australia)
I.V.A. Richards (West Indies)
C.H. Lloyd (West Indies – captain)
I.T. Botham (England)
M.J. Proctor (South Africa)
B. Taylor (England – wicketkeeper)
D.L. Underwood (England)
B. Statham (England)
C.E.L. Ambrose (West Indies)
A.A. Donald (South Africa)

Umpires: H.D. Bird and D.R. Shepherd

TEN

Over and Out

1997 was my final year in professional cricket, as I retired from the first-class list at the end of the season, before emigrating to South Africa and living in Kwa Zulu-Natal. My last season was memorable in many ways, not least for the kind words and presentations that were made, some publicly and others privately, as I made my way around the county grounds for the last time. For Gloucestershire, the final month of the season brought deep sorrow, as Diana, Princess of Wales, the county's former Patron, was killed in a car crash in Paris. Some three weeks or so after her tragic death I stood in my final game – Gloucestershire v. Lancashire at Bristol – where Jack Russell, was still wearing his black armband in memory of a fine lady.

There could have been no more fitting way to hang up my coat than to stand at the County Ground with Jackie Bond, who himself was also retiring at the end of the season after many years of distinguished service as a player with Lancashire and Nottinghamshire, and then as a coach and an umpire. Our paths had crossed many, many times before as players and umpires and, after the match finished, on 21 September – with Lancashire 9 wickets down and dourly hanging on for a draw – Jackie and I walked off with a guard of honour from the two teams.

My long-standing friend John Higson – the chairman of Gloucestershire CCC – also arranged a magnificent farewell dinner in our honour, and 100 guests were invited, including many of my former county colleagues, plus family and friends. Speeches were also made by Tony Brown, with whom I had played for Gloucestershire and who also worked as an umpire with the TCCB, before David Foot – a fine writer and local journalist – recalled some of my deeds on both the cricket and football fields of the West Country.

**GLOUCESTERSHIRE COUNTY CRICKET
CLUB**

"OVER AND NOT OUT"

A DINNER TO MARK THE RETIREMENT OF

**BARRIE MEYER
and
JACK BOND**

*In the Grace Room, Royal and SunAlliance County Ground,
Nevil Road, Bristol*

on

FRIDAY 19TH SEPTEMBER 1997

David's words were very flattering and among the many funny stories he recounted was the one about my knack of putting the ball both in the back of the net at Eastville and high over the crossbar and out of the ground. This particular story concerned Howard Radford, our goalkeeper, who lived close to the ground behind the Muller Road End and after one game met up with me in the car park and said, 'Barrie, don't worry about those balls that you kicked over the crossbar last Saturday. I've got all six of them in the boot of my car, and I'm bringing them back to the club!'

But the evening was not all about my career, as the dinner also paid tribute to Jackie Bond's career. There were also several officials from Lancashire, including their chairman Jack Simmons, who had driven down from Manchester. Jackie was given some superb glassware, while I was presented with a CD player, a handsome silver plate and a digital bedside clock radio. It was a superb send-off for both of us from our clubs, and I really appreciated the enormous effort that everyone had put into making it such a memorable occasion, especially by John Higson and his late wife Yvonne.

Not only was this wonderful evening a fine send-off, but it was a reminder that the game of cricket is still full of great sportsmanship and camaraderie. During my career in cricket, many changes had taken place – the introduction of one-day cricket, floodlit cricket and fielding restrictions, while off the field there were now third umpires, match referees and TV umpires. Many changes had taken place as well to the kit, with the advent of coloured clothing, heavier bats, lighter pads and more robust protection, including chest protectors. A far cry indeed from the days of the 1950s when I started playing club and ground and then Second XI cricket, but I'm glad to say that the friendly spirit between the players and officials is still there and, although some intense battles take place out in the middle, there are still smiles and handshakes galore off the field.

From my armchair in Natal I've also noticed over the past few years how times have changed in professional football as well. In watching the Premiership matches for only a few minutes, I'm reminded how different football has become, especially as far as discipline is concerned. There are now yellow cards and red cards in abundance yet, in my time when I played in the Football League, I only witnessed two players sent off – and then both in the same game.

There are massive wages and enormous transfers, while there are some players who frequently appear in the gossip columns for what they have allegedly done off the field. I don't have first-hand knowledge of the modern training regimes but, in my own time, when Bristol Rovers were in the Third and then the Second Division, this was the weekly training system for the first-team squad: Saturday – play a match; Sunday and Monday – report to the ground for baths and massage; Tuesday – full practice match; Wednesday – day off (I would invariably play golf); Thursday – a full morning of training, with plenty of ball work, running and other exercise drills; Friday – if we were away, morning walk, followed by a chat from the management and then travel to the match, but if we were home, we would have a light run-out and then a chat from the management.

Back in the 1950s and 1960s I was rubbing shoulders with several other footballers who were excellent cricketers and, on the county circuit, there were a host of players who, in the winter, played a good standard of League or non-League football. Today, this is simply not possible; it's one thing or the other. I can only imagine the outcry from the football managers if some of their players did not report for pre-season training in August because they were playing county cricket! Looking back, I'm just so glad that I had the chance to play both to a professional standard, as I don't know now which I would have chosen. Football was always my first love, but cricket became such a large part of my life, allowed me to travel to so many wonderful places and meet so many nice people.

I was also fortunate in that, throughout my professional career as a sportsman, I suffered very few major injuries. Injuries are inevitable when you are playing a contact sport such as football, or if you are involved with a game that involves a bit of leather flying around at great speed. I picked up several little injuries, but I was lucky enough to never have had a serious injury, and I have to thank my lucky stars that I escaped any nasty breaks.

So there have been many changes in the two sports that have been at the heart of my life, out here in South Africa and back home in England. There's certainly much more money around for the professional sportsmen of the modern era, and sponsors seem to be falling over themselves to get involved, both with teams and individual players. But I don't think I would have changed anything in my sporting life, especially as back in the 1950s and 1960s I could play both football and cricket to a professional level.

As far as umpiring is concerned, the modern Test umpire is under a lot of pressure, what with the advent of television cameras, super slow-motion replays and a certain amount of gamesmanship. The umpire's word is still final, but watching some international games recently on television from my home in South Africa, it's been clear that players – whether they are batters or bowlers – do appear sometimes to be trying it on. That's another reason why I'm perfectly happy to have done what I did while standing in the white coat – doing the job to the best of my ability, and ensuring that the game was played in the right spirit. I was pleased, too, that I was able to help oversee the introduction of new technology as the game of professional cricket moved into the modern, technological age. I don't know what some of the great umpires of the past would have made of having to use the new light meters, or having to refer close line decisions to a third umpire who was off the field and watching a TV screen. But there's one thing that I do know for sure – these gadgets and innovations will allow umpires of the future, like I hope I did throughout my time as a first-class umpire, to continue getting it right.

ELEVEN

Barrie Meyer – A Statistical Review

(With thanks to Keith Gerrish, Mike Jay, Ray Taylor, Philip Bailey and Peter Griffiths)

Full name: Barrie John Meyer
Born: 21 August 1932 in Bournemouth, Hampshire

Cricket: Right-handed batsman, wicketkeeper and occasional leg-break bowler
Football: Inside forward/centreforward

Playing Career as a Footballer:

Football League debut: 7 October, 1950 – Bristol Rovers *v.* Bournemouth
Final Football League match: 16 April 1963 – Bristol City *v.* Southend United
Major teams played for: Bristol Rovers (amateur on 13 August 1949, turning professional in November 1949) 1950/51-1957/58; Plymouth Argyle (transferred for £4,500) 1958/59; Newport County (transferred for £4,000) 1958/59-1960/61; Bristol City (transferred for £850) 1961/62-1962/63; Hereford United: 1963/64-1965/66; Glastonbury 1966/67-1967/68.

Football League record:

Bristol Rovers

Season	Appearances	Goals
1950/51	2	1
1951/52	5	1
1952/53	0	0
1953/54	27	8
1954/55	20	10
1955/56	40	20
1956/57	21	11
1957/58	24	9
Total	139	60

Plymouth Argle

Season	Appearances	Goals
1958/59	8	5

Newport County

Appearances	Goals
70	27

Bristol City

Appearances	Goals
11	8

Playing Career as a Cricketer (1957-1971)

First first-class match: Gloucestershire *v.* Essex at Gidea Park, Romford, 29 May 1957

Last first-class match: Gloucestershire *v.* Sussex at Bristol, 8 September 1971

First one-day match: Gloucestershire *v.* Middlesex at Bristol, 22 May 1963 (Gillette Cup)

Last one-day match: Gloucestershire *v.* Sussex at Hove, 5 September 1971 (Sunday League)

First-Class Career Record:

Batting and Fielding (for Gloucestershire 1957-1971)

M	I	NO	Runs	HS	Ave	100/50	Ct/St
406	569	191	5,371	63	14.20	0/11	707/119

Bowling

Balls	Mdns	Runs	Wkts	BB	Ave
30	1	28	0	–	–

One-Day Career Record:

Batting and Fielding (for Gloucestershire 1963-1971)

M	I	NO	Runs	HS	Ave	100/50	Ct/St
44	25	5	134	21	6.70	–/–	47/5

Season by Season Record in First-Class Cricket

Season	M	I	NO	Runs	HS	Ave	100/50	Ct/St
1957	7	13	3	107	30*	10.70	0/0	6/0
1958	32	43	11	382	60	11.93	0/1	30/11
1959	31	46	18	474	63	16.92	0/1	53/13
1960	31	45	7	524	61	13.78	0/2	64/10
1961	31	57	16	676	52	16.48	0/1	59/10
1962	32	49	17	624	63	19.50	0/2	50/9
1963	30	45	10	619	52	17.68	0/1	55/10
1964	32	54	11	476	63	11.06	0/1	59/16
1965	31	39	16	272	20*	11.82	0/0	47/9
1966	30	38	18	244	31*	12.20	0/0	64/7
1967	26	37	14	303	24*	13.17	0/0	46/2
1968	30	36	14	236	55*	10.72	0/1	59/2
1969	21	18	13	68	21*	13.60	0/0	34/5
1970	24	27	13	163	34	11.64	0/0	43/8
1971	18	22	10	203	55*	16.91	0/1	38/7

First–Class Fielding Record Against Each Opponent

Opponent	M	Ct/St
Australians	3	4/0
Cambridge University	5	6/2
Derbyshire	18	36/5
Essex	20	44/7
Glamorgan	25	48/8
Hampshire	27	46/8
Indians	1	1/0
Kent	21	27/10
Lancashire	20	43/5
Leicestershire	20	36/5
MCC	1	2/0
Middlesex	18	23/12
New Zealanders	2	1/0
Northamptonshire	22	35/12
Nottinghamshire	19	26/3
Oxford University	15	17/6
Pakistanis	2	4/1
Somerset	28	64/7
South Africans	2	2/0
Surrey	25	35/5
Sussex	27	58/3
Warwickshire	27	44/3
West Indians	4	9/0
Worcestershire	27	51/5
Yorkshire	27	45/12

Career as a First–Class Umpire in England:

Stood in 465 first-class matches and 450 List A one-day matches.
Stood in 26 Test matches and 23 one-day internationals.

First first-class match: Cambridge University *v.* Yorkshire at Fenner's, 28 April 1973
Last first-class match: Gloucestershire *v.* Lancashire at Bristol, 18 September 1997

First one-day match: Oxford University *v.* Warwickshire at The Parks,
  7 May 1973 (B&H Cup)
Last one-day match: Yorkshire *v.* Kent at Headingley, 14 September 1997
  (Sunday League)

Stood as an Umpire in the Following Test Matches:

24-28 June 1982	Second Test	England *v.* India at Old Trafford, with Dickie Bird
26-31 August 1982	Third Test	England *v.* Pakistan at Headingley, with David Constant
28 July-1 Aug 1983	Second Test	England *v.* New Zealand at Headingley, with David Constant
25-29 Aug 1983	Fourth Test	England *v.* New Zealand at Trent Bridge, with Dickie Bird
14-18 June 1984	First Test	England *v.* West Indies at Edgbaston, with Dickie Bird
28 June-3 July 1984	Second Test	England *v.* West Indies at Lord's, with David Evans
9-14 Aug 1984	Fifth Test	England *v.* West Indies at The Oval, with David Constant
13-18 June 1985	First Test	England *v.* Australia at Leeds, with Ken Palmer
3-8 July 1986	Third Test	England *v.* India at Edgbaston, with Dickie Bird
4-9 June 1987	First Test	England *v.* Pakistan at Old Trafford, with Dickie Bird
23-28 July 1987	Fourth Test	England *v.* Pakistan at Edgbaston, with Alan Whitehead
27 July-1 Aug 1989	Fourth Test	England *v.* Australia at Old Trafford, with John Hampshire
5-11 July 1990	Third Test	England *v.* New Zealand at Edgbaston, with John Holder
20-24 June 1991	Second Test	England *v.* West Indies at Lord's, with Ken Palmer
4-8 June 1992	First Test	England *v.* Pakistan at Edgbaston, with Merv Kitchen

| 1-6 July 1993 | Third Test | England *v.* Australia at Trent Bridge, with Roy Palmer |
| 19-23 August 1993 | Sixth Test | England *v.* Australia at The Oval, with Merv Kitchen |

Stood as an Umpire in the Following One-Day Internationals:

2 June 1977	Prudential Trophy – England *v.* Australia at Old Trafford, with David Constant
17 July 1978	Prudential Trophy – England *v.* New Zealand at Old Trafford, with Dickie Bird
9 June 1979	World Cup – England *v.* Australia at Lord's, with David Constant
13 June 1979	World Cup – England *v.* Canada at Old Trafford, with John Langridge
16 June 1979	World Cup – New Zealand *v.* West Indies at Trent Bridge, with Dickie Bird
23 June 1979	World Cup final – England *v.* West Indies at Lord's, with Dickie Bird
28 May 1980	Prudential Trophy – England *v.* West Indies at Headingley, with Ken Palmer
8 June 1981	Prudential Trophy – England *v.* Australia at Headingley, with Ken Palmer
4 June 1982	Prudential Trophy – England *v.* India at The Oval, with David Evans
9 June 1983	World Cup – England *v.* New Zealand at The Oval, with Don Oslear
13 June 1983	World Cup – England *v.* Pakistan at Lord's, with Alan Whitehead
15 June 1983	World Cup – India *v.* West Indies at The Oval, with David Shepherd
18 June 1983	World Cup – India *v.* Zimbabwe at Tunbridge Wells with Merv Kitchen
25 June 1983	World Cup final – India *v.* West Indies at Lord's, with Dickie Bird
4 June 1984	Texaco Trophy – England *v.* West Indies at Lord's, with David Evans

3 June 1985   Texaco Trophy – England *v.* Australia at Lord's, with
                   Dickie Bird

16 July 1986   Texaco Trophy – England *v.* New Zealand at
                   Headingley, with Jack Birkenshaw

23 May 1987   Texaco Trophy – England *v.* Pakistan at Trent Bridge,
                   with David Constant

19 May 1988   Texaco Trophy – England *v.* West Indies at Edgbaston,
                   with Jack Birkenshaw

29 May 1989   Texaco Trophy – England *v.* Australia at Lord's, with
                   David Shepherd

23 May 1990   Texaco Trophy – England *v.* New Zealand at
                   Headingley, with Nigel Plews

20 May 1992   Texaco Trophy – England *v.* Pakistan at Lord's, with
                   David Shepherd

19 May 1993   Texaco Trophy – England *v.* Australia at Old Trafford,
                   with David Shepherd

Stood as an Umpire in the Following Major One-Day Games in the UK:

13 June 1973   Benson & Hedges Cup   Hampshire *v.* Kent at
                                              Southampton, with Eddie
                                              Phillipson

1 August 1973   Gillette Cup   Sussex *v.* Kent at Hove,
                   quarter-final   with Peter Wight

12 June 1974   Benson & Hedges Cup   Kent *v.* Leicestershire at
                   quarter-final   Canterbury, with Ron Aspinall

31 July 1974   Gillette Cup   Yorkshire *v.* Lancashire at
                   quarter-final   Headingley, with Hugo
                                              Yarnold

4 June 1975   Benson & Hedges Cup   Middlesex *v.*
                   quarter-final   Yorkshire at Lord's, with
                                              Henry Horton

6 August 1975   Gillette Cup   Nottinghamshire *v.*
                   quarter-final   Derbyshire at Trent Bridge,
                                              with Arthur Fagg

23 June 1976   Benson & Hedges Cup   Warwickshire *v.*
                   semi-final   Worcestershire at Edgbaston,
                                              with Ken Palmer

8 June 1977	Benson & Hedges Cup quarter-final	Northamptonshire *v.* Warwickshire at Northampton, with Bill Alley
2 September 1978	Gillette Cup final	Somerset *v.* Sussex at Lord's, with Dickie Bird
6 June 1979	Benson & Hedges Cup quarter-final	Middlesex *v.* Yorkshire at Lord's with Peter Wight
21 July 1979	Benson & Hedges Cup final	Essex *v.* Surrey at Lord's, with Dickie Bird
8 August 1979	Gillette Cup quarter-final	Northamptonshire *v.* Leicestershire at Northampton, with Alan Whitehead
19 July 1980	Benson & Hedges Cup final	Essex *v.* Northamptonshire at Lord's, with David Constant
25 July 1981	Benson & Hedges Cup final	Somerset *v.* Surrey at Lord's, with Dickie Bird
5 August 1981	NatWest Trophy quarter-final	Derbyshire *v.* Nottinghamshire at Derby, with Ken Palmer
16 June 1982	Benson & Hedges Cup quarter-final	Nottinghamshire *v.* Leicestershire at Trent Bridge, with Bill Alley
4 August 1982	NatWest Trophy quarter-final	Hampshire *v.* Surrey at Southampton, with Bill Alley
4 September 1982	NatWest Trophy final	Surrey *v.* Warwickshire at Lord's, with Dickie Bird
1 June 1983	Benson & Hedges Cup quarter-final	Lancashire *v.* Northamptonshire at Old Trafford, with Don Oslear
23 July 1983	Benson & Hedges Cup final	Middlesex *v.* Essex at Lord's, with Dickie Bird
1 September 1984	NatWest Trophy final	Middlesex *v.* Kent at Lord's, with Dickie Bird

5, 7 June 1985	Benson & Hedges Cup quarter-final	Essex *v.* Derbyshire at Chelmsford, with Alan Whitehead
21 August 1985	NatWest Trophy semi-final	Hampshire *v.* Essex at Southampton, with Nigel Plews
7 September 1985	NatWest Trophy final	Essex *v.* Nottinghamshire at Lord's, with David Constant
11 June 1986	Benson & Hedges Cup semi-final	Worcestershire *v.* Kent at Worcester, with Barrie Leadbeater
27 May 1987	Benson & Hedges Cup quarter-final	Yorkshire *v.* Hampshire at Headingley, with Don Oslear
12 August 1987	NatWest Trophy semi-final	Leicestershire *v.* Northamptonshire at Leicester, with Kevin Lyons
8 June 1988	Benson & Hedges Cup semi-final	Glamorgan *v.* Derbyshire at Swansea, with Barrie Leadbeater
10 August 1988	NatWest Trophy semi-final	Surrey *v.* Middlesex at The Oval, with Jack Birkenshaw
17 September 1989	Refuge Assurance Cup final	Essex *v.* Nottinghamshire at Edgbaston, with John Holder
30 May 1990	Benson & Hedges Cup quarter-final	Somerset *v.* Middlesex at Taunton, with Kevin Lyons
15th August 1990	NatWest Trophy semi-final	Lancashire *v.* Middlesex at Old Trafford, with David Constant
29 May 1991	Benson & Hedges Cup quarter-final	Yorkshire *v.* Warwickshire at Headingley, with Chris Balderstone
31 July 1991	NatWest Trophyl quarter-final	Warwickshire *v.* Somerset at Edgbaston, with Kevin Lyons

1 September 1991	Refuge Assurance Cup semi-final	Lancashire *v.* Northamptonshire at Old Trafford, with David Constant
27 May 1992	Benson & Hedges Cup quarter-final	Surrey *v.* Lancashire at The Oval, with Merv Kitchen
12 August 1992	NatWest Trophy semi-final	Warwickshire *v.* Northamptonshire at Edgbaston, with Ken Palmer
10 July 1993	Benson & Hedges Cup final	Derbyshire *v.* Lancashire at Lord's, with David Shepherd
28 July 1993	NatWest Trophy quarter-final	Glamorgan *v.* Worcestershire at Swansea, with Ray Julian
9 August 1994	NatWest Trophy semi-final	Warwickshire *v.* Kent at Edgbaston, with John Hampshire
30 May 1995	Benson & Hedges Cup quarter-final	Lancashire *v.* Nottinghamshire at Old Trafford, with John Holder
13 August 1996	NatWest Trophy semi-final	Surrey *v.* Essex at The Oval, with Roy Palmer
27 May 1997	Benson & Hedges Cup quarter-final	Yorkshire *v.* Northamptonshire at Headingley, with Nigel Plews

Index

If you are interested in purchasing other books published by Tempus,
or in case you have difficulty finding any Tempus books in your local bookshop,
you can also place orders directly through our website

www.tempus-publishing.com